MagiCORE

Reading Comprehension

NONFICTION

Standards Aligned | 10 Nonfiction Skills | Articles & Question Sets

Anchor Charts | Full Year of Practice

LEXILE

TABLE OF CONTENTS

Unit I: Key Ideas and Details

TABLE OF CONTENTS

Unit 2: Craft and Structure

TABLE OF CONTENTS

Unit 3: Integration of Knowledge and Ideas

How to Use This Resource

This resource meets Common Core and many state reading standards. It includes:

Anchor Charts: These anchor charts should be used to introduce the skills. Students can refer to journal anchor charts while completing independent work.

Anchor Charts

Model Text: The model practice page includes a shorter text with questions targeted based on the anchor chart.

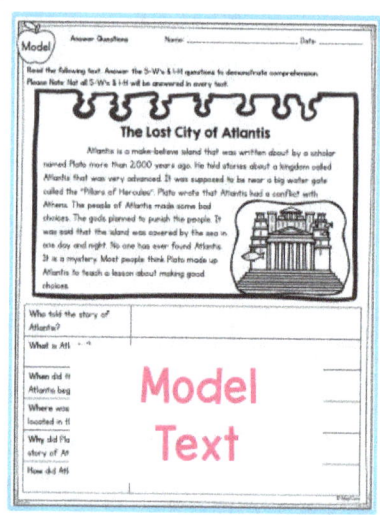

Model Text

Practice Passages: These passages are Lexile leveled and include standards-based questions. These passages should be used in order since they increase in difficulty.

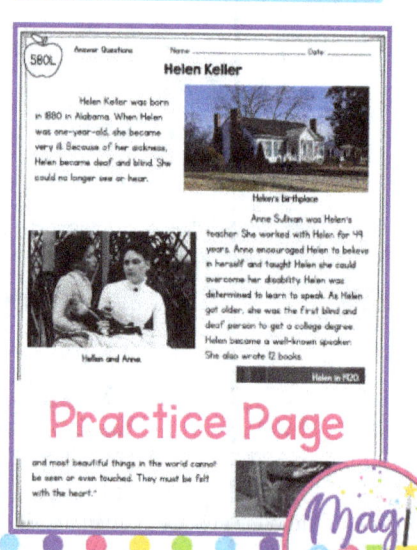

Practice Page

Assessment: One assessment passage is included. This should be used at the end of the unit to check student mastery of the topic.

MagiCORE

ABOUT LEXILE LEVELS

Common Core Kingdom, LLC DBA MagiCore® is a certified Lexile® Partner. These texts are officially measured and approved by Lexile and MetaMetrics® to ensure appropriate rigor and differentiation for students.

The Lexile Framework® for Reading measures are scientific, quantitative text levels. When the Lexile of a text is measured, specific, measurable attributes of the text are considered, including, but not limited to, word frequency, sentence length, and text cohesion. These are difficult attributes for humans to evaluate, so a computer measures them.

Common Core State Standards uses Lexile level bands as one measure of text complexity. Text complexity ranges ensure students are college and career ready by the end of 12th grade. Lexile measures help educators scaffold and differentiate instruction as well as monitor reading growth.

Grade Band	Lexile® Bands Aligned to Common Core Expectations
K-1	N/A
2-3	420L-820L
4-5	740L-1010L
6-8	925L-1185L

Keep in mind when using any leveled text that many students will need scaffolding and support to reach text at the high end of their grade band. According to Appendix A of the Common Core Standards, "It is important to recognize that scaffolding often is entirely appropriate. The expectation that scaffolding will occur with particularly challenging texts is built into the Standards' grade-by-grade text complexity expectations, for example. The general movement, however, should be toward decreasing scaffolding and increasing independence both within and across the text complexity bands defined in the Standards."

Unit 1: Key Ideas and Details

Ask and Answer Questions in Nonfiction

Topic, Main Ideas, Details

Historical, Scientific & Procedural Texts

1

ASK AND ANSWER NONFICTION QUESTIONS

The 5-W's & 1-H can help readers demonstrate understanding of key details in a text.

- People
- Animals

- Important events
- Facts and details

- Time
- Sequence

- Place

- Reasons
- Cause

- Details or Evidence

TYPES OF QUESTIONS

While reading, you can ask and answer explicit or implicit questions to monitor your comprehension.

Explicit

"Right There" Questions

- The answer can be found right in the text.

- Don't try to remember the answer. You may get tricked!

- Underline the <u>answer</u> in the text. Don't underline other things!

Text

Text + My Brain

Implicit or Inferential

- The answer will <u>not</u> be in the text.
- There will be <u>text evidence</u> to help you make an inference.
- You need to <u>think</u> about the answer.

3

Model

Read the following text. Answer the 5-W's & I-H questions to demonstrate comprehension. Please Note: Not all 5-W's & I-H will be answered in every text.

The Lost City of Atlantis

Atlantis is a make-believe island that was written about by a scholar named Plato more than 2,000 years ago. He told stories about a kingdom called Atlantis that was very advanced. It was supposed to be near a big water gate called the "Pillars of Hercules". Plato wrote that Atlantis had a conflict with Athens. The people of Atlantis made some bad choices. The gods planned to punish the people. It was said that the island was covered by the sea in one day and night. No one has ever found Atlantis. It is a mystery. Most people think Plato made up Atlantis to teach a lesson about making good choices.

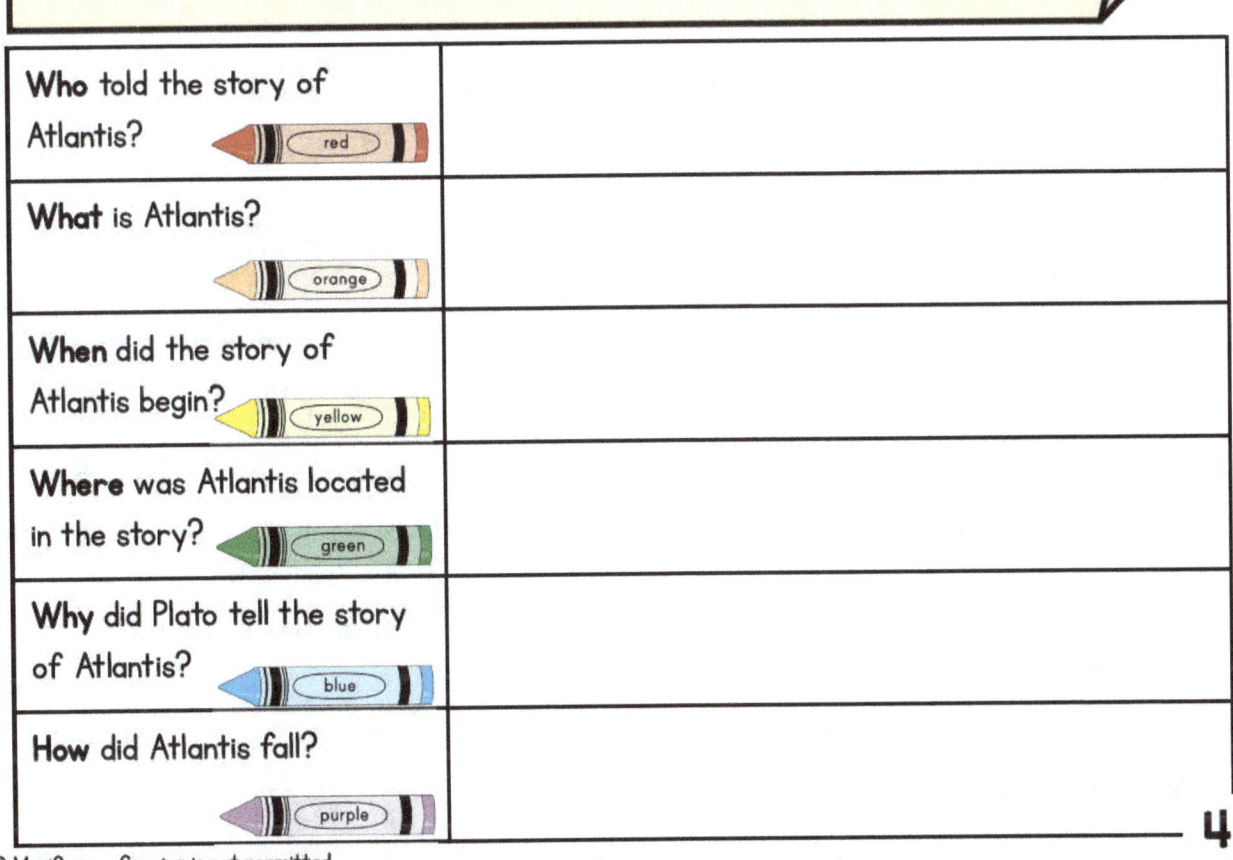

Who told the story of Atlantis? _red_	
What is Atlantis? _orange_	
When did the story of Atlantis begin? _yellow_	
Where was Atlantis located in the story? _green_	
Why did Plato tell the story of Atlantis? _blue_	
How did Atlantis fall? _purple_	

480L

How to Learn Sign Language

Imagine not being able to hear any sounds around you. You would never learn what language sounds like. Some people are deaf. This means they cannot hear. Some deaf people talk by using sign language. Follow these steps to learn sign language.

1.   Check out a sign language book from your library.

2.   Learn the signs for the alphabet letters. Once you know the alphabet, you will be able to spell any word.

3.   Take your time when you sign. This will make it easier for someone to understand you.

4.   Practice with a partner.

5.   Learn signs for basic words such as "hello" and "how are you?"

6.   Continue to learn more vocabulary.

7.   You can always watch videos on the internet.

The ASL (American Sign Language) Alphabet

Learning sign language is not easy. You can learn the basics, so you are able to speak with deaf people.

5

Name: _____ Date: _____

Answer the following Questions. <u>Underline</u> the text evidence in the color indicated.

1. What does *deaf* mean?   red

_____

_____

2. How could you start learning sign language?   orange

_____

_____

_____

3. Why should you learn to sign for the alphabet before signing words?

    a.   Letters are the easiest signs to learn.   yellow

    b.   Once you know the letters, you can spell words.

    c.   You can practice with a partner.

    d.   Learning sign language is not easy.

4. When should you learn harder vocabulary?   green

    a.   Before you learn the alphabet.

    b.   After you learn the alphabet.

    c.   Before you learn basic vocabulary.

    d.   After you learn basic vocabulary.

5. Why is it important to take your time when you are learning to sign?

    blue

_____

_____

_____

6. What can you do if you are having trouble learning sign language?

purple

_____

_____

_____

7. Why was sign language invented?

pink

_____

_____

_____

8. Who would learn sign language? (Circle all that apply.)

brown

a.   A college student who studies reading.

b.   A deaf child.

c.   Someone with a friend who cannot hear.

d.   Someone interested in learning different languages.

9. Ask your own who, what, when, where, why, or how question about the text. Write the answer to the question below.

black

Question:

_____

_____

Answer:

_____

_____

7

Helen Keller

Helen's birthplace

Helen Keller was born in 1880 in Alabama. When Helen was one-year-old, she became very ill. Because of her sickness, Helen became deaf and blind. She could no longer see or hear.

Anne Sullivan was Helen's teacher. She worked with Helen for 49 years. Anne encouraged Helen to believe in herself and taught Helen she could overcome her disability. Helen was determined to learn to speak. As Helen got older, she was the first blind and deaf person to get a college degree. Helen became a well-known speaker. She also wrote 12 books.

Hellen and Anne

There are movies and plays about Helen. Her birthplace is a museum. Helen helped change the way the world sees people with disabilities. She also spoke out for women's rights. As Helen once said, "The best and most beautiful things in the world cannot be seen or even touched. They must be felt with the heart."

Helen in 1920

Answer Questions   Name: _____   Date: _____

Answer the following Questions. <u>Underline</u> the text evidence in the color indicated.

1. Where was Helen born?   `red`

_____

_____

2. Why did Helen become deaf and blind?   `orange`

_____

_____

3. Who was Helen's teacher?   `yellow`

_____

_____

4. When did Helen become deaf and blind?   `green`

   a.   When she was born.

   b.   After her illness

   c.   After she learned to speak.

   d.   Before she graduated college.

5. What were some of Helen's accomplishments?   `blue`

   a.   Helen wrote 12 books.

   b.   Helen starred in a movie and play

   c.   Helen graduated college.

   d.   Helen became a speaker.

9

6. How did Anne Sullivan help Helen?   `purple`

_____

_____

7. What does Helen's quote *"The best and most beautiful things in the world cannot be seen or even touched. They must be felt with the heart"* mean?   `pink`

_____

_____

_____

8. Why is it important to remember Helen today?   `brown`
- a.   She has movies and plays about her.
- b.   Helen was deaf and blind.
- c.   Helen got a college degree.
- d.   Helen helped change the way people see others with disabilities.

9. Ask your own who, what, when, where, why, or how question about the text. Write the answer to the question below.   `black`

Question:

_____

_____

Answer:

_____

_____

640L

The Human Body

The human body is an amazing machine! There are many parts that work together that make you see, think, feel and move.

Without your brain, you could not live. Your brain is the control station that sends your body messages to think, feel, and move. For example, if you touch a hot stove, a message is sent to your brain to tell you to move your hand before you get burnt.

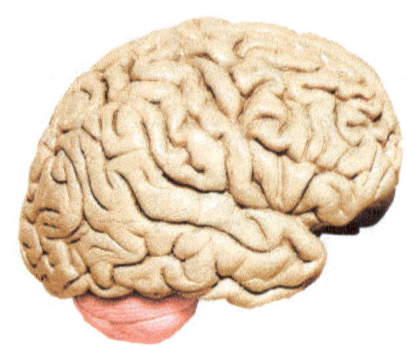

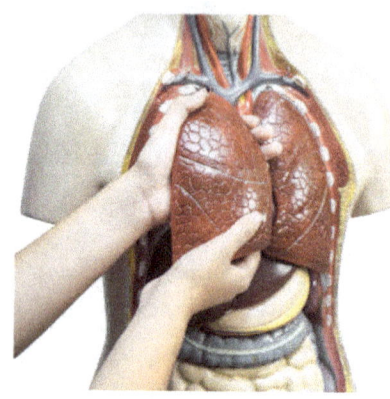

Your lungs are in your chest. They help you breathe. You breathe in oxygen from the air. The air is then moved through your blood. Your lungs also remove carbon dioxide from your body.

Did you know that your heart is a muscle? Your heart is the organ that pumps blood through your body. Blood also moves oxygen and nutrients to all the parts of your body. Blood travels through your body in arteries and veins.

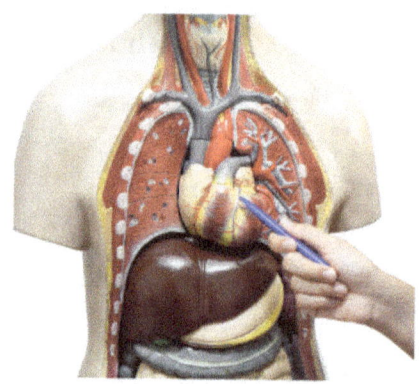

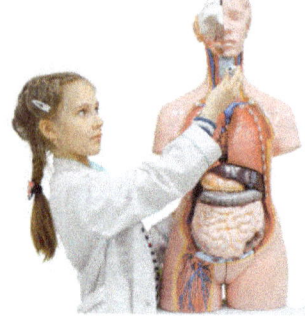

Each organ in your body works together to help you live.

ll

Answer the following Questions. <u>Underline</u> the text evidence in the color indicated.

1. What does your brain do?   red

_____

_____

2. Why are your lungs important?   orange

_____

_____

3. How do the lungs and the heart work together?   yellow

    a.   The lungs take in oxygen, then the heart turns the oxygen into carbon dioxide.

    b.   The lungs take in oxygen, which is then pumped through blood by the heart.

    c.   The lungs bring blood to your heart.

    d.   The lungs are a muscle that helps your heart make you think, feel, and move.

4. How does blood carry oxygen and nutrients through your body?   green

    a.   Blood carries oxygen and nutrients through your brain.

    b.   Blood carries oxygen and nutrients through your lungs.

    c.   Blood carries oxygen and nutrients through your heart.

    d.   Blood carries oxygen and nutrients through your veins and arteries.

                                         blue

5. Where are your lungs?

_____

_____

12

Name: _____ Date: _____

6. Why is your heart important?   purple

_____

_____

_____

7. What would happen if your heart stopped working?   pink

_____

_____

_____

8. Why does the author call your body a machine?   brown

    a.   because all of your body parts work together

    b.   because your heart and lungs work together

    c.   because without your organs you could not think, feel, and move

    d.   because your heart is a muscle

9. Ask your own who, what, when, where, why, or how question about the text. Write the answer to the question below.   black

Question:

_____

_____

Answer:

_____

_____

13

690L

How to Brush Your Teeth

It is important to brush your teeth correctly. Brushing your teeth will prevent cavities and other gum diseases. To brush your teeth, follow these simple steps:

1. Wet your toothbrush.

2. Squeeze toothpaste onto your toothbrush so it covers the bristles.

3. Gently brush each tooth in a circular motion. Be sure to brush the front, back, and top of your teeth.

4. Be sure to reach your brush far back so you don't miss any teeth.

5. Spit the foam and saliva from brushing into the sink.

6. Spend at least three minutes brushing your teeth.

To have healthy gums and clean teeth, be sure to brush two times every day. The best times to brush are after breakfast and before bed.

14

Name: _____ Date: _____

Answer the following Questions. <u>Underline</u> the text evidence in the color indicated.

1. Why should you brush your teeth?

red

_____

_____

2. What should you do before you put toothpaste on the toothbrush?

orange

_____

_____

3. When should you brush the front, back, and top of your teeth?

yellow

    a.   Before you put toothpaste on the brush

    b.   After you put toothpaste on the brush.

    c.   Before you wet your toothbrush.

    d.   After you wet your toothbrush children

4. Why should you reach your brush far back?

green

    a.   to brush your tongue

    b.   to brush your gums

    c.   to brush the top of your mouth

    d.   to reach your back teeth

5. How long should you brush your teeth?

blue

_____

_____

_____

Answer Questions Name: ______________________________ Date: __________________

6. Where should you brush?

purple

____

____

____

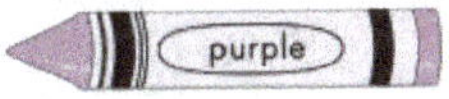

7. What should you do when your mouth gets full of foam?

pink

____

____

____

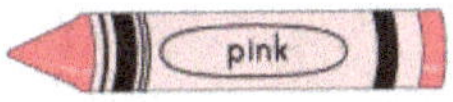

8. What might happen if you did not brush your teeth? (Circle all that apply.)

brown

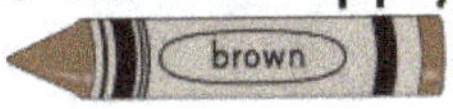

a. You would rot.

b. Your teeth would turn red.

c. Your tongue would fall out.

d. Your breath would smell bad.

9. Ask your own who, what, when, where, why, or how question about the text. Write the answer to the question below.

black

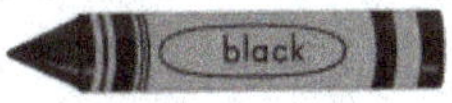

Question:

____

____

Answer:

____

____

580L

TEST: A Healthy Addition to Your Diet

What is leafy green, crispy, tasty, and can be used in a variety of meals? Spinach! Spinach is the best food ever.

Spinach is the best food. It is super healthy. Did you know spinach is packed with vitamins and fiber? Spinach will keep you strong and healthy like Popeye.

Spinach is an awesome vegetable. It can be used in a variety of ways. Spinach can be eaten raw in a salad. It can be cooked as a side. Don't like cooked spinach? Try it on a pizza. Still don't like the taste of this leafy green? Try blending spinach in a smoothie with bananas and orange juice. You won't even taste it. Spinach is a very versatile vegetable that you can add to any meal.

Spinach is a super food because you can grow it yourself. Growing spinach in your garden is easy. Simply plant the seeds in dirt and water it regularly. Then you will be able to pick this amazing vegetable any time you want!

Spinach truly is an amazing and versatile vegetable. It is fun to find creative ways to put this leafy green into your meals.

17

Name: _____ Date: _____

Answer the following Questions. <u>Underline</u> the text evidence in the color indicated.

1. What is the author's opinion in this text?   [red crayon: red]

_____

_____

2. When can you eat spinach?   [orange crayon: orange]

_____

_____

3. How do you know spinach is healthy?   [yellow crayon: yellow]

    a.   Spinach is tasty.

    b.   Popeye loves spinach.

    c.   Spinach can be cooked.

    d.   Spinach is packed with vitamins and fiber.

4. What reasons does the author give to support their opinion?

    a.   Spinach can be used in a variety of ways.   [green crayon: green]

    b.   Spinach is green.

    c.   Spinach tastes sweet and delicious.

    d.   You can grow your own spinach.

5. What can you do if you don't like cooked spinach?   [blue crayon: blue]

_____

_____

18

6. Why does the author call spinach a super food?

purple

_____

_____

7. Why would a person put spinach in a smoothie?

pink

_____

_____

_____

8. What is another way the author may suggest you use spinach?

   a.   in your ice cream

   b.   on a cheeseburger instead of lettuce

   c.   give it to your dog

   d.   mixed in cookie dough instead of chocolate chips

brown

9. Ask your own who, what, when, where, why, or how question about the text. Write the answer to the question below.

black

Question:

_____

_____

Answer:

_____

_____

TOPIC

What is the whole text about in a short word or phrase?

 Look for words or phrases that are repeated.

MAIN IDEA

What is the whole text about?
The main idea should be a sentence.

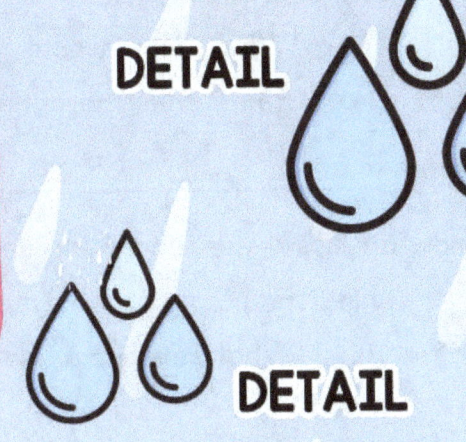

DETAIL

DETAIL

DETAIL

DETAILS:

What reasons or evidence does the author give to support the point?

Model

Read the following text. Complete the following questions to help you determine the topic, main idea, and supporting details. Color text evidence using the color crayon shown.

Unwrapping the Truth of Fortune Cookies

Fortune cookies are fun treats that hold a surprise message inside. But did you know they come with their own mystery about where they started? Many people think fortune cookies were first made in China, but actually, they were created in the United States! In the early 1900s, people in San Francisco and Los Angeles started making these cookies. They were inspired by Japanese cookies that also had messages inside. Fortune cookies quickly became a special part of eating out at Chinese restaurants in America. Inside each cookie, you find a piece of paper with a fortune or a wise saying. Even though fortune cookies weren't really from China, these cookies became famous around the world. Fortune cookies are a fun way to end a meal with a bit of luck and laughter.

1. How do I find the **main topic** of a text?
   red
   - Look for words or phrases that are **repeated**. The topic should be a word or short phrase that the whole text is about.

Main Topic: _____

2. How do I find the **main idea** of a text?
   orange
   - Ask, "What is the whole text about?" The main idea should be a sentence.
   - Note: Sometimes the text will tell you the main idea, but not always!

Main Idea: _____

3. How do I find the **supporting details** in a text?
   yellow
   - Find the portion of the text where the author makes the point.
   - Ask. "What reasons or details does the author give to support the point?"

Supporting Details:

_____

470L

The Amish Way of Life

The Amish are a group of people living in America. They live very simply. The Amish speak their own language. Over 165,000 Amish live in the United States. 1,500 Amish live in Canada. The Amish population is growing. 80% of Amish people live in Pennsylvania.

The Amish have strict rules. The church makes rules. Electricity, phones, and cars are not allowed. People use horses and buggies. Women wear long dresses with aprons. Men wear pants, shirts, and suspenders. They wear plain colors. People who do not follow rules are shunned. Being shunned means they are rejected by their community. They need to make up for their wrongdoings. Amish who do not make up for their wrongdoings are excommunicated. Excommunicated members are thrown out of their community.

The Amish community has their own schools. Many of these schools are one-room schoolhouses. A teacher teaches all ages in one classroom. Unmarried Amish women teach Amish schools. There are about 30 children in a class. Children learn English, reading, writing, math, and history. Children go to school until 8th grade. After, they help their family with household duties.

An Amish woman

Amish women take care of their family. They also take care of the church and community. Amish women cook. They make and wash clothes. They help neighbors. Amish women follow their husbands. Amish men are often farmers. They grow crops and raise livestock. Amish use horses on their farms.

The Amish way of life is different from modern Americans. Despite this, the Amish thrive. They have a strong community. They take care of each other.

An Amish family on a buggy

Topic, Main Ideas, Details   Name: _____ Date: _____

Answer the following questions. <u>Underline</u> the text evidence in the color indicated.

1. What is the topic of this text?   `red`

    a.   Amish people

    b.   Where Amish live

    c.   Amish schools

    d.   Amish rules

2. Which sentence best tells the main idea of this text?   `orange`

    a.   The Amish have very strict rules.

    b.   The Amish have very simple lives.

    c.   The Amish focus their lives around their family and community.

    d.   The Amish people have a different way of life from modern Americans.

3. What details helped you determine the main idea?   `yellow`

_____

_____

4. What is the main idea of paragraph 2?   `green`

_____

_____

5. Which detail could the author add to paragraph 4 to support the main idea? (Choose all that apply).   `blue`

    a.   Some Amish men are carpenters.

    b.   Amish children often walk to school.

    c.   Amish women are responsible for caring for children.

    d.   Amish people gather in their homes to practice their religion.

6. What is the main idea of paragraph 4?   `purple`

    a.   Amish men and women have different roles.

    b.   The Amish community has their own schools.

    c.   Amish women are responsible for their family.

    d.   The Amish way of life is different than people who live in modern America.

23

Mercury

Mercury is the closest planet to the sun. Mercury is named after a Roman god. A year on Mercury lasts 88 earth days. Mercury completes a rotation once every two years. Therefore, Mercury has only one day in two earth years! A day on Mercury is twice as long as a year on Earth!

Mercury is the smallest planet in our solar system. Mercury is rocky. The rocks make this planet gray. Mercury has craters. Craters make it look like the moon. The craters are caused by comets and asteroids. Mercury has no rings or moons. The temperature on Mercury varies. It can be as cold as -280 degrees Fahrenheit at night. It can be as warm as 800 degrees Fahrenheit during the day. There is no atmosphere. This means that there is no weather on Mercury.

Two spacecraft have visited Mercury. In 1970, Mariner 10 flew by Mercury. Mariner 10 took pictures. These pictures helped us understand Mercury's surface, atmosphere, and temperature. In 2004, Messenger flew around Mercury more than 4,000 times. It mapped the planet. This spacecraft also discovered ice on Mercury. Messenger ran out of fuel. It crashed into the planet. We still have a lot to learn about Mercury. You can see Mercury from earth at times. The best times to look are morning or evening.

Mariner 10 launch

View of Mercury from Mariner 10

Answer the following questions. <u>Underline</u> the text evidence in the color indicated.

1. What is the topic of this text?   `red`
   - a. Space
   - b. Mercury
   - c. Planets in our solar system
   - d. Mercury and Earth

2. Which sentence best tells the main idea of this text?   `orange`
   - a. Mercury is closest to the sun.
   - b. Two spacecraft visited Mercury.
   - c. There is a lot to learn about Mercury.
   - d. Planets are interesting to learn about.

3. What details helped you determine the main idea?   `yellow`

   _____

   _____

4. What is the main idea of paragraph 2?   `green`
   - a. What Mercury looks like and its climate.
   - b. Mercury looks similar to the moon.
   - c. Mercury's temperature can be very cold or very hot.
   - d. Mariner 10 took photographs of Mercury.

5. What is the main idea of paragraph 3?

   _____

   _____

6. What is the main idea of paragraph 4?   `blue`
   - a. Amish men and women have different roles.
   - b. The Amish community has their own schools.
   - c. Amish women are responsible for their family.
   - d. The Amish way of life is different than people who live in modern America.

25

Harriet Tubman

Harriet Tubman was born in 1822 in Maryland. She was a slave. When Harriet was five years old, her job was to take care of her owner's baby. When she got older, she worked in the fields.

In 1849 Harriet escaped slavery. She fled to Pennsylvania. The journey was 90 miles. Harriet returned to Maryland to rescue her family. After, she continued to help other slaves. She made about thirteen trips. Harriet rescued around 70 slaves. She traveled at night to avoid being caught. Slave owners were furious. They offered rewards for her capture. After she rescued slaves, Harriet helped them find work. She took them as far North as Canada.

During the US Civil War, Harriet worked for the Union Army. The Union Army fought for the northern and southern states to stay together. Northern states were free states. Southern states were slave states. Harriet worked for the Union Army as a cook and nurse. She also guided an attack. The attack freed more than 700 slaves.

After the Union won the Civil War, Harriet moved to New York. She took care of her parents. She worked for women's right to vote. Harriet got very sick. She died in 1913.

Harriet is still remembered for her work during slavery and the Civil War. She was a courageous hero. She risked her life to help others.

Harriet Tubman in 1880

Topic, Main Ideas, Details   Name: _____ Date: _____

Answer the following questions. <u>Underline</u> the text evidence in the color indicated.

1. What is the topic of this text? Use text evidence to support your answer.

`[red]`

_____

_____

2. Which sentence best tells the main idea of this text?

`[orange]`

    a.   Harriet Tubman escaped slavery.

    b.   Harriet Tubman saved many slaves.

    c.   Harriet Tubman helped the Union Army.

    d.   Harriet Tubman did many important things throughout her life.

3. What details helped you determine the main idea?

`[yellow]`

_____

_____

4. What is the main idea of paragraph 1?

`[green]`

_____

_____

5. Based on the text, how could you describe Harriet Tubman? (Choose all that apply).

`[blue]`

    a.   brave

    b.   heroic

    c.   fearful

    d.   Daring

6. What is the main idea of paragraph 3?

`[purple]`

    a.   Harriet led an attack.

    b.   Harriet freed 700 slaves.

    c.   Harriet worked for the Union Army.

    d.   Northern states were free states and southern states were slave states.

27

600L

Bears

Bears are mammals that live in different habitats around the world. Different species of bears live in different habitats. Bears have been around since prehistoric times. Humans have hunted them for their meat and fur. Today, bears are threatened because humans are destroying their habitats.

Brown bears are the largest land predators. They live in northern Europe, Asia, and North America. Brown bears are not always brown. Brown bears in India are red. In North America, they can be a cream color to almost black. They have long and thick fur. They also have large claws. Brown bears are unable to climb trees because their claws are dull. Brown bears range in size and can weigh between 120 to 1,500 pounds.

Brown Bear

Black Bear

The American Black Bear lives in North America. They are the smallest and most common bear in North America. Black bears are not always black. They can be white, blond, or brown. They live in large forests., but sometimes they leave the woods to search for food. They can enter areas people live in to search for food. Black bears can open doors and jars. They are powerful. They can weigh between 90 and 550 pounds. Black bears are omnivores. They eat both plants and animals.

The polar bear lives in the Arctic Circle. Along with some brown bears, they are the largest land predator. Polar bears can weigh 770-1,500 pounds. Polar bears are white. They have large feet. Their feet help them walk on snow and ice and to swim. Most polar bears are born on land, but they spend most of their time in

Polar Bear

the ocean. Polar bears are carnivores. Their main food source is seals.

Polar bears have adapted to cold temperatures. They have a thick layer of fat that keeps them warm. Polar bears are endangered. Climate change threatens polar bears. The ice they live on is melting. Pollution is also a threat to polar bear's survival.

There are many different types of bears. Their habitats, physical features, and temperaments vary. It is important to learn about these amazing animals so we can help minimize the impact humans have on them.

TYPES OF BEARS

Panda Bear   Polar Bear   Brown Bear   Black Bear

Answer the following questions. <u>Underline</u> the text evidence in the color indicated.

1. What is the topic of this text? Use text evidence to support your answer.   `red`

_____

_____

2. Which sentence best tells the main idea of this text?   `orange`

    a.   Bears are many different colors.

    b.   There are different types of bears.

    c.   Humans are taking over the habitats of bears.

    d.   Brown bears and polar bears are the largest land mammals.

3. What details helped you determine the main idea?   `yellow`

_____

_____

4. What is the main idea of paragraph 2?   `green`

_____

_____

5. What is the main idea of paragraph 4?   `blue`

    a.   Polar bears are white.

    b.   Polar bears live in the arctic circle.

    c.   Polar bears are endangered.

    d.   Polar bears have interesting characteristics.

6. According to the author, why should we learn about bears?   `purple`

    a.   Bears can be dangerous.

    b.   Bears are very interesting.

    c.   There are many different types of bears.

    d.   We can reduce the effect we have on bears and their habitats

30

730L

How to Make Pancakes

I love waking up to the mouthwatering smell of homemade pancakes.
Follow these steps to make this simple and classic breakfast for your family.

Ingredients
- 1 ½ cups flour
- 3 ½ teaspoons baking power
- 1 teaspoon salt
- 1 tablespoon sugar
- 1 ¼ cups milk
- 1 egg
- 3 tablespoons melted butter

1. First, sift together all of the dry ingredients (flour, baking powder, salt, sugar).

2. Next, add the milk, egg, and melted butter. Mix until the batter is smooth.

3. Mix chocolate chips or blueberries into the batter (optional).

4. Turn a frying pan on medium heat. Add a small amount of cooking oil or butter to the pan to prevent sticking.

5. Then, scoop about ¼ cup of batter into the middle of the frying pan.

6. Allow the pancake to cook until you see bubbles forming.

7. After, flip the pancake. Cook until brown.

8. Repeat steps 4-6 until you have made all of the pancakes.

9. Enjoy your pancakes warm with butter and maple syrup.

31

Answer the following questions. <u>Underline</u> the text evidence in the color indicated.

1. What is the topic of this text? Use text evidence to support your answer.   `red`

_____

_____

2. Which sentence best tells the main idea of this text?   `orange`

    a.   Pancakes are delicious.

    b.   Pancakes have a lot of ingredients.

    c.   It is simple to learn how to make pancakes.

    d.   Everyone should eat pancakes for breakfast.

3. What details helped you determine the main idea?   `yellow`

_____

_____

4. What would happen if you skipped step 3?   `green`

_____

_____

5. What should you do after you flip the pancake?   `blue`

    a.   Make all of the pancakes.

    b.   Watch for bubbles to form.

    c.   Scoop ¼ cup of batter onto the pan.

    d.   Add cooking oil or butter to the pan to prevent sticking.

6. What should you do after you add the wet ingredients?   `purple`

    a.   Sift the dry ingredients.

    b.   Turn the frying pan on medium heat.

    c.   Mix in chocolate chips or blueberries.

    d.   Stir the ingredients until they are smooth.

800L

The Super Bowl is the final professional football game of the season. This championship game determines the best NFL team. The game currently falls on the first Sunday in February.

History of The Super Bowl

The first Super Bowl was on January 15, 1967. Super Bowl I was played in Los Angeles, California. The team that wins the big game gets the Vince Lombardi Trophy. This trophy is named after a Green Bay Packers coach. Vince Lombardi led his team to the first two Super Bowl victories. The Pittsburgh Steelers have held the most Super Bowl wins with six victories. The Dallas Cowboys and the San Francisco 49ers each have five victories.

Super Bowl's Importance in America

Super Bowl Sunday has become a part of American culture. It has been one of the most-watched television programs of the year. The Super Bowl is the second largest day for food, second to Thanksgiving. Super Bowl commercials have become a huge attraction as well. These commercial slots are the most expensive of the

President Reagan congratulates New York Giants after Super Bowl XXI win in 1987

year. Companies come up with clever commercials that are almost as entertaining as the game itself. The halftime show is a large part of The Super Bowl as well. Famous musicians such as Michael Jackson and Madonna have performed.

Throughout history, the Super Bowl's importance has grown in America. It has become the most watched sporting event in the United States.

33

Topic, Main Ideas, Details   Name: _____ Date: _____

Answer the following questions. <u>Underline</u> the text evidence in the color indicated.

1. What would be a good title for this text?   `red`

    a.   American Culture

    b.   Professional Football

    c.   The Super Bowl Championship

    d.   Sporting Events on Television

2. Which sentence best tells the main idea of this text?   `orange`

    a.   The Super Bowl's importance has grown in America.

    b.   The first Super Bowl was played on January 15, 1967.

    c.   The Super Bowl determines the best NFL team of the season.

    d.   The Super Bowl is the final professional football game played every year.

3. What details helped you determine the main idea?   `yellow`

_____

_____

4. What is the main idea of paragraph 2?   `green`

_____

_____

5. Which details could be added to support the main idea of paragraph 2?
(Choose all that apply).   `blue`

    a.   The name Super Bowl came from Lamar Hunt.

    b.   There are four NFL teams that have never played in the Super Bowl.

    c.   When the Super Bowl first started, it was a championship between the NFL and AFL.

    d.   The Green Bay Packers, New York Giants, and New England Patriots have won four Super Bowl championships.

6. What is the main idea of paragraph 3?   `purple`

    a.   The Super Bowl has been occurring for a long time.

    b.   The Super Bowl has become a part of American culture.

    c.   Famous musicians perform at the Super Bowl halftime show.

    d.   Food and commercials are a large part of the Super Bowl celebration.

34

670L

TEST: The Tower of London

The Tower of London is an old historic castle. It is next to the River Thames in London. This castle was founded in 1066. It holds a lot of history for the city of London.

The Tower of London used to be a grand palace. There are numerous buildings surrounded by defensive walls and a moat. Royals lived here. Kings Richard the Lionheart, Henry III, and Edward I expanded this palace.

Outside View of the Tower of London

Prison in the Tower

The castle was also used as a fortress. Guns were placed around the castle. Weapons and ammunition were stored here as well.

The Tower of London was used as a prison from 1100 to 1952. Elizabeth I was a prisoner here before she became queen. During World War I and World War II, the tower was used as a prison for spies.

During World War II, bombs damaged the castle and destroyed buildings. After World War II, the castle was repaired and reopened to the public.

Visitors of London flock to the Tower of London. It is one of the most popular tourist attractions. Over 2 million people visit each year! Visitors to the castle can see royal armor and the Crown Jewels. The Crown Jewels are crowns worn by previous and current royalty. The Tower of London is now a protected World Heritage Site.

Crown Jewels

35

Answer the following questions. <u>Underline</u> **the text evidence in the color indicated.**

1. What is the topic of this text? Use text evidence to support your answer.

red

_____

_____

2. Which sentence best tells the main idea of this text?

orange

    a.   The Tower of London was used as a prison.

    b.   The Tower of London houses the Crown Jewels.

    c.   The Tower of London is a popular tourist destination.

    d.   The Tower of London is important to the history of London.

3. What details helped you determine the main idea?

yellow

_____

_____

4. What is the main idea of paragraph 2?

green

_____

_____

5. Which detail could the author add to paragraph 4 to support the main idea that *The Tower of London was used as a prison*? (Choose all that apply)

blue

    a.   Six Ravens still live at the tower today.

    b.   Anne Boleyn was also a prisoner at The Tower.

    c.   There was once a collection of wild animals at The Tower.

    d.   Seven people were killed in the tower before World War I.

6. What is the main idea of paragraph 6?

purple

    a.   The Tower of London was once a prison.

    b.   The Tower of London is a popular tourist attraction.

    c.   The Crown Jewels can be seen at the Tower of London.

    d.   Bombs struck the Tower of London during World War II.

36

Historical Texts

Historical texts are informational texts about people, places, and events in history. Historical texts often explain *why* events happened. People read historical texts to learn about the past and how it affected the future.

You can understand how historical events are connected through cause and effect relationships.

Cause and Effect Relationships

Cause: WHY something happens
- Something happens be<u>CAUSE</u> of something else.

Effect: WHAT happens
- The end result.

To explain relationships between historical texts, ask yourself:
1. What happened?
2. Why did this happen?

Effect: What happened

On August 28, 1963, Martin Luther King Jr. and others participated in the March on Washington to stand up for civil rights for African Americans.

Cause: Why it happened

African Americans were discriminated against. They did not have the same rights as white Americans.

37

Model

Answer the following questions. <u>Underline</u> the text evidence in the color indicated.

The Great Extinction

Long ago, dinosaurs roamed the Earth. They had many advantages like big bodies, sharp teeth, and quick speeds for hunting and protecting themselves. However, about 66 million years ago, a huge asteroid hit the Earth. This caused dust and ash to block the sun for a long time, making it much colder and darker than usual. Because of this sudden change, plants struggled to grow, and many animals couldn't find enough food. As a result, even the mighty dinosaurs couldn't survive. They eventually became extinct.

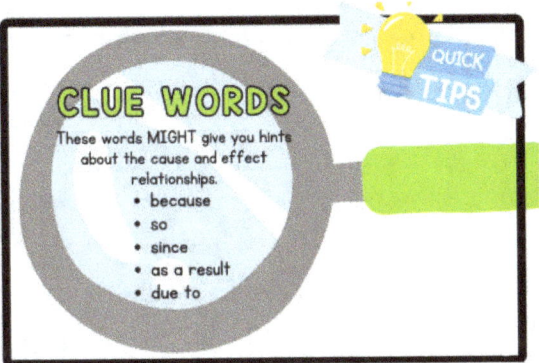

1. What happened 66 million years ago?

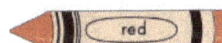

_____

_____

2. What happened due to the asteroid? (Hint: look for clue words.)

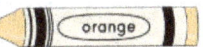

_____

_____

3. Why did dinosaurs go extinct?

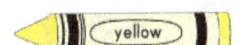

_____

_____

520L

The History of Memphis, Tennessee

Memphis is a city in Tennessee. Its history began thousands of years ago. It was settled by the Mississippian Culture. The Mississippian Culture was a Native American tribe.

In 1541 the Europeans began exploring this area. Hernando de Soto was one of the first explorers to visit this area.

The Mississippian Culture was a mound-building culture.

Memphis is located where the dot is on the map.

Memphis became a city in 1819. The founders named this city after the ancient capital of Egypt. The land was fertile. Large plantations were built. These plantations used slaves to keep up with their demands. As a result, the city became a major trading center for cotton.

In 1878 and 1879 a horrible disease called Yellow Fever spread through Memphis. Thousands of residents left the city. More than 5,000 people died. Because of this, the city became broke. The city eventually recovered. Memphis is thriving city today.

Memphis today

39

Answer the following questions. Underline **the text evidence in the color indicated.**

I. Which event caused Memphis to become a city?   `red`

    a.   Europeans began exploring the area.

    b.   Yellow fever killed thousands of people.

    c.   It was settled by the Mississippian culture.

    d.   The city was named after the ancient capital of Egypt.

2. Why were large plantations built?   `orange`

_____

_____

3. What caused Memphis to become a major trading center for cotton?   `yellow`

_____

_____

4. What happened as a result of yellow fever? (Choose all that apply.)   `green`

    a.   Large plantations were built.

    b.   Thousands of residents left.

    c.   More than 5,000 people died.

    d.   The city became a major trading center for cotton.

5. Why did Memphis become broke?   `blue`

_____

_____

6. Fill in one cause and effect event below: `purple`

Cause		Effect
	→	

680L

Amelia Earhart

    Amelia Mary Earhart was born on July 24, 1897. She was the first female **aviator** to fly solo across the Atlantic Ocean. She received the **U.S. Distinguished Flying Cross** since she broke this record. She set many other records. She also wrote bestselling books about her flying experiences. Earhart made an **attempt** to fly around the earth in 1937. She disappeared over the Pacific Ocean near Howland Island. Amelia Earhart's disappearance remains a mystery. **Fascination** with her life, career, and disappearance continues to this day.

aviator – *pilot*   **U.S. Distinguished Flying Cross**– *award*   **attempt** – *try*
fascination – *interest*

41

Answer the following questions. <u>Underline</u> the text evidence in the color indicated.

1. Why did Amelia Earhart earn the Distinguished Flying Cross? ◄ ▭ red ▭

    a.   She set many records.

    b.   Amelia Mary Earhart was born on July 24, 1897.

    c.   She also wrote bestselling books about her flying experiences.

    d.   She was the first female **aviator** to fly solo across the Atlantic Ocean.

2. What happened to Amelia when she attempted to make a flight around the globe?   ▭ orange ▭

_____

_____

3. Why is Amelia Earhart remembered today?   ▭ yellow ▭

a.   She visited Howard Island.

b.   Earhart made an **attempt** to fly around the earth in 1937.

c.   People are fascinated with her life, career, and disappearance.

d.   She also wrote bestselling books about her flying experiences.

4. What does the photograph show?   ▭ green ▭

_____

_____

5. Fill in one cause and effect event below   ▭ blue ▭

Cause	Effect

Scientific Texts

Scientific texts are informational texts that tell facts and scientific ideas. People read scientific texts to understand scientific topics.

Some scientific ideas are connected through compare and contrast relationships.

Compare & Contrast Relationships

Compare: how topics or ideas a similar

Contrast: how topics or ideas are different

To explain relationships between compare and contrast scientific texts, ask yourself:

1. How are these topics or ideas similar?
2. How are these topics or ideas different?

Compare:

How are tornados and thunderstorms similar?

Contrast:

How are tornados and thunderstorms different?

43

Compare & Contrast Clue Words

Clue words can help you determine how the author connects events, ideas, concepts, or procedures. Clue words will NOT always be in the text, so do not rely on clue words along.

COMPARE CLUE WORDS
How things are similar.
like same, both, the same as, similar, in the same way, similarly, as, too, have in common, as well as

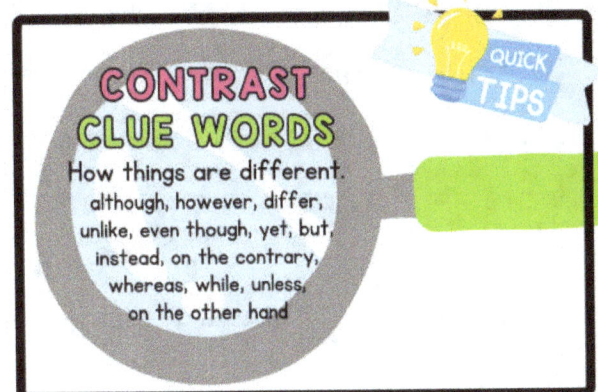

CONTRAST CLUE WORDS
How things are different.
although, however, differ, unlike, even though, yet, but, instead, on the contrary, whereas, while, unless, on the other hand

Read the paragraph below.
Highlight the COMPARE key words
Highlight the CONTRAST key words

    In 1912, the Titanic left on its maiden voyage. The ship was the first of its kind, yet it tragically sank after hitting an iceberg. This event showed the limits of human technology and the need for safety. In contrast, the first moon landing in 1969 showcased technology's potential to break boundaries. Astronauts walked on the moon. This event turned a dream into reality and opening a new chapter in space exploration. Both events were important, but while the Titanic's voyage highlighted the importance of safety, the moon landing celebrated human curiosity and invention. Through both stories, we learn from the past and are inspired to face the future.

470L

States of Water

Water can exist in three different states: solids, liquids, or gases. Water in the solid state is called ice. Ice has a set shape. Ice can appear **translucent**. Water is a liquid. Water is a liquid because it can be poured. Unlike ice, water takes the shape of the container it is in. Similar to ice, liquid water is translucent. Water vapor is water in its **gaseous** state. On the contrary to ice and water, water vapor is invisible. It cannot be seen. Like liquid water, water vapor takes the shape of the container it is in.

translucent: mostly see through
gaseous: being a gas

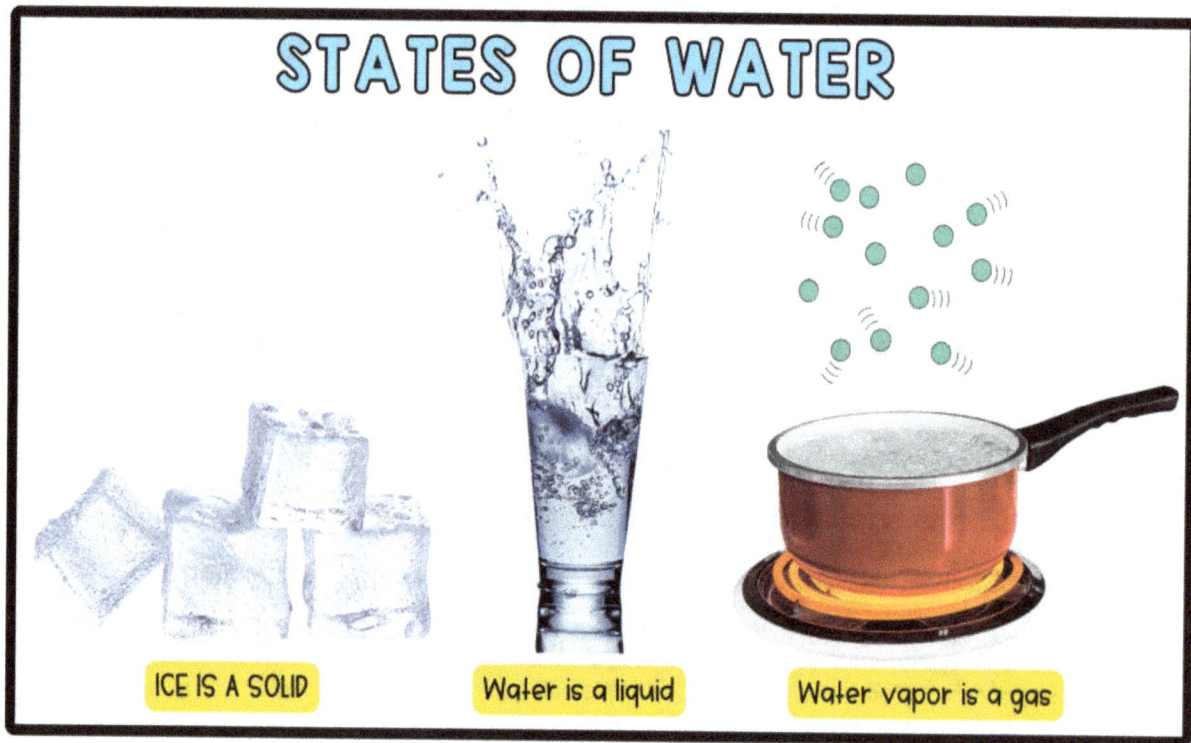

STATES OF WATER

ICE IS A SOLID   Water is a liquid   Water vapor is a gas

Name: _____ Date: _____

Answer the following questions. <u>Underline</u> the text evidence in the color indicated.

1. How are ice and water alike?   `red`

      a.   Ice and water have a set shape.

      b.   Ice and water cannot be seen.

      c.   Similar to ice, liquid water is translucent.

      d.   Unlike ice, water takes the shape of the container it is in.

2. How are ice and water different?   `orange`

_____

_____

_____

_____

3. How are water and water vapor alike?   `yellow`

      a.   Water and water vapor are invisible.

      b.   Similar to ice, liquid water is translucent.

      c.   Water and water vapor are liquids that can be poured.

      d.   Like liquid water, water vapor takes the shape of the container it is in.

4. How are ice and water vapor different?   `green`

_____

_____

_____

_____

_____

540L

Bees vs. Ants

Bees and ants have many similarities and differences. Both insects live in colonies with others of their species. Similarly, they both have queens. The queens lead the colonies and workers. Also, both insects have six legs. In addition, bees and ants hatch

The Queen Bee is marked with the blue dot.

from eggs as larvae. After, it becomes a pupa. Eventually, they molt. They become full-grown bees or ants. Both of these bugs may be considered pests, but they actually help people. Ants clean up the environment. They eat harmful insects and help plants grow. Bees pollinate flowers. They also make honey.

Queen Ant

On the contrary, bees and ants have some differences. They look different. Bees are typically yellow and black, but ants are often black or red. Bees make their own food, while ants find their food. Bees live in hives, whereas ants live in the ground. There are about 15,000 species of ants. There are about 1,000 species of bees.

1. How are bees and ants alike? (Compare)

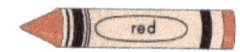
red

_____

_____

_____

2. How are bees and ants different? (Contrast)

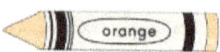
orange

_____

_____

_____

47

Procedural Texts

Procedural texts are informational texts that tell how to complete tasks. A set of directions is a type of procedural text. Directions are often written in steps, or procedures. The steps are sometimes accompanied by diagrams or pictures to help the reader complete the steps.

Procedural texts are written in ==sequential order.==

Sequential Order

Tells the order, or sequence, you should follow.

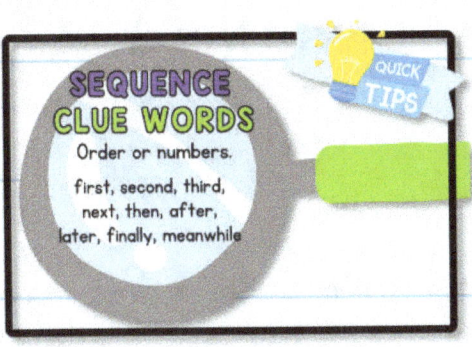

SEQUENCE CLUE WORDS
Order or numbers.
first, second, third, next, then, after, later, finally, meanwhile

QUICK TIPS

While reading procedural texts, ask yourself:

1.   What are the directions telling me to do?
2.   Why are the directions telling me to do each step?

How to Make a Peanut Butter and Jelly Sandwich

1. Gather ingredients

2. Spread 1 tbsp. of peanut butter onto the bread.

3. Spread 1 tbsp. of jelly onto the bread.

4. Put the two slices of bread together.

5. Enjoy!

580L

How to Bathe a Dog

Is your dog stinky? Is your dog constantly tracking dirt and mud into the house? Follow these simple steps to clean your pooch.

Materials
- dog shampoo
- towel
- bathtub
- dog treats

1. First, gather all of your materials so that they are close at hand. Turn the water on for a few minutes to get it to a warm temperature.

2. Next, bring your dog into the tub. Encourage him or her with a treat.

3. After that, wet your dog's fur thoroughly. Be sure to wet his or her face, but avoid getting water in their eyes.

4. Then, gently massage shampoo into your dog's fur. Don't forget his or her ears and paws!

5. Finally, rinse your dog with water until there is no soap left.

6. Last, dry your dog with a towel. Give him or her a treat for good behavior.

49

Procedural Steps   Name: _____ Date: _____

Answer the following questions. <u>Underline</u> the text evidence in the color indicated.

1. What task do these directions tell you how to do?   `red`

_____

_____

2. How do you know when to do these steps?   `orange`

_____

_____

3. What should you do before you bring your dog into the tub? Why?

                                        `yellow`

_____

_____

4. What should you do as you bring your dog into the tub?   `green`

    a.   Gather all of your materials.

    b.   Encourage him or her with a treat.

    c.   After that, wet your dog's fur thoroughly.

    d.   Turn the water on for a few minutes to get it to a warm temperature.

5. What should you do after you wet your dog's fur?   `blue`

    a.   Gently massage shampoo into your dog's fur.

    b.   Rinse your dog with water until there is no soap left.

    c.   Dry your dog with a towel.

    d.   Give him or her a treat for good behavior.

6. What would happen if you skipped step 6?   `purple`

_____

_____

7. How do the pictures help you understand what to do?   `brown`

_____

50

640L

How to Make Witch Hat Cookies

Do you want to make a cute and festive snack for a Halloween party? Follow these simple steps. You'll have your guests begging for more!

Materials
- Fudge Stripes cookies
- Hershey's Kisses
- Orange frosting

1. First, lay a Fudge Stripes Cookie on a plate. The chocolate side should be facing up.

2. Next, carefully spread orange frosting over the hole of the Fudge Stripes cookie.

3. Then, unwrap a Hershey's Kiss. Place the bottom of the Hershey's Kiss over the frosting on the Fudge Stripes cookie. Wipe away any smeared frosting.

4. You may draw a bow around the Hershey' Kiss. It will make it look like a bow on the hat. This is optional.

5. Repeat steps 1-4 until you have made all of the witch hats you need.

6. Last, allow the frosting on the witch hats to dry.

I hope your party guests enjoy this fun and festive Halloween treat!

51

Answer the following questions. <u>Underline</u> the text evidence in the color indicated.

1. What is this text about?   red

    a.   It is a non-fiction text about Halloween.

    b.   It is a story about delicious Halloween snacks.

    c.   It is a non-fiction text about cause and effect.

    d.   It is a procedural text about how to make a cookie witch hat.

2. What key words from the text help you know when to do the steps?   orange

    a.   first, next, then

    b.   because, so, since

    c.   ay, carefully, unwrap

    d.   second, after that, last but not least

3. What should you do before you place the bottom of the Hershey's Kiss over the frosting?   yellow

    a.   Allow the frosting to dry.

    b.   Unwrap the Hershey's Kiss.

    c.   Draw a bow around the Hershey's Kiss.

    d.   Lay the Fudge Stripes cookie with the fudge facing down on the plate.

4. What should you do after you have made all of the witch hats you need?   green

    a.   Eat them.

    b.   Repeat steps 1-4.

    c.   Allow the frosting to dry.

    d.   Draw a bow around the Hershey's Kiss.

5. Why did the author include the 2nd picture?   blue

    a.   To show you how delicious the cookies will taste

    b.   To show you how to put the frosting on the cookie

    c.   To show you how to draw the bow on the witch hat

    d.   To show you what the witch hat cookies should look like

6. What would happen if you skipped step 4?   purple

    a.   The witch hats will have no top.

    b.   The witch hats will not have a bow.

    c.   The witch hats will look really funny.

    d.   The witch hats will not come out right.

52

Unit 2: Craft & Structure

Context Clues in Nonfiction

Nonfiction Text Features

Author's Purpose

Be a Word Detective!

Context Clues

Clues in a text that can help me figure out what a word means.

Not all words have Context Clues.

Sometimes Context Clues are not clear enough to fully understand the word meaning.

What are Context Clues?

- Look right after the word.
- Look in the sentence before the word.
- Look in the sentence after the word.

Next...

1. Replace the unknown word with the new word.
2. Ask yourself, "Does the new word make sense?"

What to do if there aren't Context Clues.

- Look up the word in a dictionary or online dictionary
- As a friend or adult

WORD DETECTIVES USE CONTEXT CLUES

Definition (meaning)

The <u>concept</u>, or idea, was new to her.

Examples

The <u>data</u>, such as reading level growth, can be found in student binders.

*like
*such as
*or

Word Parts

Is there a helpful prefix, suffix, or root word?

helpful

rewrite

pretest

Synonyms (Same)

The turtle <u>sauntered</u> slowly through the grass.

Antonyms (Opposite)

The plate wasn't brittle because it did not break when she dropped it on the floor.

Model

Read the following text. Find the context clues to determine the meaning of each bold word.

The Wonders of the Rainforest

Rainforests are **teeming** with life. They are filled with many types of plants and animals. In these dense jungles, you can find creatures ranging from **miniscule** insects to large mammals. Every part of the forest is **bustling** with activity, unlike the **desolate** deserts.

One fascinating plant is the **epiphyte**, which grows on other trees instead of in the soil. This type of plant, such as orchids and ferns, uses its host for support. This is a **symbiotic** relationship benefiting both organisms. Epiphytes can better access sunlight, and they don't harm their host.

Word	Color the Context Clue	Type of Context Clue	Word Meaning
teeming	red		
miniscule	orange		
bustling	yellow		
desolate	green		
epiphyte	blue		
symbiotic	purple		

540L

How Chocolate Is Made

A favorite treat of many people is chocolate. Whether it is in cookies, cakes, candies, or drinks, most people love this **decadent** and delicious sweet. Have you ever wondered where chocolate comes from?

Chocolate begins by growing in cocoa pods. Farmers **harvest** these pods twice a year. When harvested, the cocoa pods are picked and cut open. A white pulp that has the cocoa beans inside is taken out. Next, the pulp is **fermented** in containers. This is when the pulp and beans are left out to break down. Fermentation helps develop the flavor of the chocolate.

Farmer harvesting cocoa pod

After five to seven days of fermentation, the cocoa beans are dried in the sun. Next, the beans are shipped all over the world to **chocolatiers**.

Once the chocolatier receives the beans, he or she **roasts** them. Some chocolatiers roast their beans in ovens. Next, the cocoa beans have their shells removed. This process is called **winnowing**. The cocoa nib is left. Then, the coca nibs are ground into a paste. Soon after, sugar is added to the chocolate. Milk powder can also be added to make milk chocolate. Afterward, the chocolate is **tempered**. Tempering is when the temperature of the chocolate is raised and lowered to create crystals. This makes the chocolate shiny and firm. Most chocolatiers have a machine that does this.

White pulp inside cocoa pod

Cocoa beans being dried

Lastly, the chocolate is poured into a mold. The mold can be shaped like a chocolate bar, hearts for Valentine's Day, or a bunny for Easter.

58

Context Clues   Name: _____ Date: _____

Answer the following questions. <u>Underline</u> the text evidence in the color indicated.

1. What is the meaning of "decadent" in the first paragraph of the passage?

     a.   sour

     b.   bitter

     c.   delightful

     d.   Chocolaty

(red)

2. Read these sentences from paragraph 2 of the passage:

*Farmers **harvest** these pods twice a year. When harvested, the cocoa pods are picked and cut open.*

What does the word "harvest" mean in paragraph 2? (Pick all that apply.)

     a.   chop

     b.   pick

     c.   gather

     d.   grow

(orange)

3. What is the meaning of the word "fermented" in paragraph 2?

(yellow)

_____

_____

4. What is the meaning of the word "chocolatiers" in paragraph 3?

(green)

_____

_____

5. Read these sentences from paragraph 4 of the passage:

*Once the chocolatier receives the beans, he or she **roasts** them. Some chocolatiers roast their beans in ovens.*

What does the word "roast" mean in paragraph 4?

(blue)

_____

_____

6. What is the meaning of the word "winnowing" in paragraph 4?

(purple)

     a.   The chocolate is poured into a mold.

     b.   The shells are removed from the cocoa bean.

     c.   Sugar and milk powder are added to the cocoa paste.

     d.   The temperature of the chocolate is raised and lowered.

59

560L

The Life Cycle of a Chicken

What came first- the chicken or the egg? This famous question has **perplexed** people for centuries. It is impossible to answer this question because the life cycle of a chicken does not begin or end. It is **continuous**!

A chicken's life begins when it hatches from an egg. After about three months, the chick becomes an adult. An adult female chicken is called a **hen**. An adult male chicken is called a **rooster**.

A chick grows into a hen or rooster.

When a hen is six months old, she begins laying eggs. Up to six eggs are laid every day. If there is a rooster to fertilize the egg, the egg will eventually grow into a chick. If there is not a rooster around, this egg will never become a chick. However, it can become your breakfast!

When an egg is fertilized, it grows inside the hen for a day.

After the egg is laid, it takes 21 days for the chick to grow.

Once an egg is fertilized, the chick begins to grow inside. It starts out as a **cell** in the mother's body. A cell is a single unit of life that you can't see. The cell grows for a day until the hen lays the egg. Then the mother sits on the egg to keep it warm. This is called **brooding**.

After about 21 days, the chick is ready to hatch. A chick hatches from the egg by pecking through the shell with its beak.

A chick hatches from an egg.

60

Context Clues   Name: _____ Date: _____

Answer the following questions. <u>Underline</u> the text evidence in the color indicated.

1. What is the meaning of "perplexed" as it is used in the first paragraph of the passage?   `red`

    a.   asked

    b.   thought

    c.   confused

    d.   answered

2. Read these sentences from paragraph 1 of the passage: `orange`

*It is impossible to answer this question because the life cycle of a chicken does not begin or end. It is **continuous**!*

What does the word "continuous" mean in paragraph 1? (Pick all that apply.)

    a.   short

    b.   endless

    c.   nonstop

    d.   ongoing

3. What is the meaning of the word "hen" in paragraphs 2 and 3?   `yellow`

_____

_____

4. What is the meaning of the word "rooster" in paragraphs 2 and 3?   `green`

_____

_____

5. Read these sentences from paragraph 4 of the passage: `blue`

*It starts out as a **cell** in the mother's body. A cell is a single unit of life that you can't see. The cell grows for a day until the hen hatches the egg.*

What does the word "cell" mean in paragraph 4?

_____

_____

6. What is the meaning of the word "brooding" in paragraph 4?   `purple`

    a.   when a hen sits on an egg

    b.   when a cell grows into a chick

    c.   when an egg hatches from the shell

61   d.   when an egg grows inside of the hen

570L

A Day in My Life: Spain

My name is Esperanza Balon. I am eight years old. I live in Madrid, Spain with my mama, papa, grandma, and my little brother Carlos.

8:00 a.m.: I usually wake up around 8:00 a.m.. I eat cereal with milk and watch a show on TV. After breakfast, I get ready for school.

This is me!

My School

9:00 a.m.: My mom walks Carlos and me to school. It takes us about 20 minutes.

9:30 a.m.: School starts. My teacher is Mrs. Sanchez. There are 29 kids in my class. We learn social studies, reading, writing, **arithmetic**, art, and physical education.

12:00 p.m.: This is my favorite time of day- lunch time! Carlos and I go home for lunch with my family. My papa even comes home for lunch. My mama cooks a **massive** meal that includes an appetizer, main course, and dessert. My favorite is seafood **paella**. Paella is a dish of rice and seafood. After lunch, we take a small **siesta**, or nap.

Seafood Paella

2:30 p.m.: It's time to go back to school. We finish our lessons and end the day with physical education.

5:00 p.m.: Our school day is over. Carlos and I slowly **amble** home and do our homework.

8:00 p.m.: We have a small dinner, such as a sandwich or omelet.

10:00 p.m.: It's time for bed! I am ready for a **slumber** after a long day. I don't like to stay awake too late on a school night!

62

Answer the following questions. <u>Underline</u> the text evidence in the color indicated.

1. What is the meaning of "arithmetic" as it is used in the 4th paragraph of the passage?

     red

     a.   math

     b.   writing

     c.   reading

     d.   physical education

2. Read this sentence from paragraph 5 of the passage:

     orange

*My mama cooks us a **massive** meal that includes an appetizer, main course, and dessert.*

What does the word "massive" mean in paragraph 5? (Pick all that apply)

     a.   large

     b.   huge

     c.   small

     d.   tasty

3. What is the meaning of the word "paella" in paragraph 5?   yellow

_____

_____

4. What is the meaning of the word "siesta" in paragraph 5?   green

_____

_____

5. Read this sentence from paragraph 7 of the passage: blue

*Carlos and I slowly **amble** home and do our homework.*

What does the word "amble" mean in paragraph 7?

_____

_____

6. What is the meaning of the word "slumber" in paragraph 9?   purple

     a.   nap

     b.   sleep

     c.   snack

     d.   stories

63

600L

How to Play Go Fish

Card games are a simple and **gratifying** way to keep you and a friend entertained. Go Fish is an easy game you can play anywhere!

<u>Materials</u>
Deck of 52 cards
2-4 players

To Win: Make the most sets of alike cards.

A deck contains 52 cards.

1. Be sure you have a complete deck of 52 cards.
2. **Deal**, or pass out, five cards to each player.
3. Place the remaining cards in the center of the players.
4. Players **sort** their cards. It helps to put all of the cards with the same numbers together.
5. When a player gets all four cards in the set, he or she puts the cards down in front of him or her.
6. Each player takes a turn **requesting** a certain card he or she needs from another player. For example, player one may ask player three, "Do you have any Jacks?"
7. If the player does have the requested card, he or she **forfeits** all of the cards of that type. If the player asked does not have the card, he or she tells the player to "go fish".
8. To "go fish", the player takes a card out of the pile of cards in the center.
9. Players continue to take turns until all of the players **discard** all of their cards. No cards should be left in the middle.

    Next time you are bored, grab a deck of cards, and teach a friend to play Go Fish! This game can keep you entertained for hours!

Context Clues   Name: _____ Date: _____

Answer the following questions. <u>Underline</u> the text evidence in the color indicated.

1. What is the meaning of "gratifying" as it is used in the first paragraph of the passage?   `( red )`

    a.   boring

    b.   dreary

    c.   difficult

    d.   satisfying

2. Read this sentence from step 2 of the passage:

Deal, or pass out, five cards to each player.

What does the word "deal" mean in step 2? (Pick all that apply.)   `( orange )`

    a.   give

    b.   take

    c.   dispense

    d.   distribute

3. What is the meaning of the word "sort" in step 4?   `( yellow )`

_____

_____

4. What is the meaning of the word "requesting" in step 6?   `( green )`

_____

_____

5. Read these sentences from step 7 of the passage: `( blue )`

*If the player does have the requested card, he or she **forfeits** all of the cards of that type. If the player asked does not have the card, he or she tells the player to "go fish".*

What does the word "forfeits" mean in step 7?

_____

_____

6. What is the meaning of the word "discard" in step 9?   `( purple )`

    a.   take

    b.   grab

    c.   share

65   d.   get rid of

730L

The Black Widow Spider

Black widow spiders are one of the most **dreaded** spiders in North America. This is because they are **venomous**, or poisonous. They are called black widows because the females usually eat their mates!

Black widow spiders are **arachnids**. Arachnids are animals with eight legs. This spider is easily recognized. It usually has a red or orange hourglass shape on its stomach. Females have shiny, dark black bodies and are about 1-2 inches long. Males are a lighter black. They are about half the size of females. Some males have red spots on their backs.

Black widows live in **moderate** climates all around the world. Areas with cold winters are too cold for them. They can be found in the southern and western parts of the United States. They are also found in South America, Southern Europe, Asia, Australia, and Africa.

Black widows eat other arachnids and various insects. Their diet includes flies, ants, mosquitoes, caterpillars, cockroaches, and grasshoppers. They trap their prey in webs. Then, they use their feet to wrap their prey in silk. Next, they injure their prey with their fangs. Finally, they inject digestive enzymes into the insects. The insect's organs liquefy. The spiders suck up the liquid. The black widow can live for months without eating. Some can live up to a year without food!

Black widows are one of the most venomous spiders to **reside** in North America. Their venom can be fifteen times stronger than rattlesnake venom! While this sounds **treacherous**, these predators will only strike humans if they are disturbed. Their bites are painful, but if they are treated, they rarely cause death.

Black Widow Spider

Context Clues   Name: _____ Date: _____

Answer the following questions. <u>Underline</u> the text evidence in the color indicated.

1. What is the meaning of "dreaded" as it is used in the first paragraph of the passage?   `red`

    a.   loved

    b.   feared

    c.   famous

    d.   interesting

2. Read these sentences from paragraph 1 of the passage: `orange`

*Black widow spiders are one of the most **dreaded** spiders in North America. This is because they are **venomous**, or poisonous.*

What does the word "venomous" mean in paragraph 1? (Pick all that apply.)

    a.   toxic

    b.   Scary

    c.   frightful

    d.   fascinating

3. What is the meaning of the word "arachnids" in paragraph 2?   `yellow`

_____

_____

4. What is the meaning of the word "moderate" in paragraph 3?   `green`

_____

_____

5. Read this sentence from paragraph 5 of the passage: `blue`

*Black widows are one of the most venomous spiders to **reside** in North America.*
What does the word "reside" mean in paragraph 5?

_____

_____

6. What is the meaning of the word "treacherous" in paragraph 5?   `purple`

    a.   safe

    b.   amazing

    c.   exciting

67   d.   dangerous

Test: The Star of the Sea

Did you know that starfish are actually not fish at all? This popular sea creature is an **invertebrate** because it does not have a backbone.

7-Legged Starfish

There are about 2,000 different **species** of starfish. They usually have 5 arms, but some types have up to 40 arms! Starfish can be smooth, bumpy, or spiny. Many starfish have bright colors. They have tube feet. Their feet help them attach to and climb sand, rocks, and coral. Tube feet help them move since starfish cannot swim. Their mouths are located underneath their body in the center. Did you know that starfish do not have brains? They also do not have blood. Their **nervous systems** are spread throughout their limbs. Their limbs communicate movements throughout their bodies.

Amazingly, starfish can **regenerate**, or regrow, limbs that become damaged or lost. Starfish may even shed arms to defend themselves from harmful predators. Predators include snails, crabs, sea turtles, otters, and birds.

Starfish feed on whatever is available to them. Some of their **diet** includes worms, snails, and larvae. Some species of starfish eat their **prey** outside of their bodies! Their stomachs can come out to digest food. Then, the stomach goes back into their bodies.

Starfish eating a mussel

Starfish have appeared in legends across cultures. Even though some starfish can be poisonous, some cultures eat these creatures.

68

Context Clues   Name: _____ Date: _____

Answer the following questions. <u>Underline</u> the text evidence in the color indicated.

1. What is the meaning of "invertebrate" as it is used in the first paragraph of the passage? *(red)*

    a.   a fish

    b.   a creature

    c.   an animal with a backbone

    d.   an animal without a backbone

2. Read these sentences from paragraph 2 of the passage: *(orange)*

*There are about 2,000 different **species** of starfish. They usually have 5 arms, but some types have up to 40 arms!*

What does the word "species" mean in paragraph 2? (Pick all that apply.)

    a.   fish

    b.   kinds

    c.   types

    d.   varieties

3. What is the meaning of the word "nervous systems" in paragraph 2? *(yellow)*

_____

_____

4. What is the meaning of the word "regenerate" in paragraph 3? *(green)*

_____

_____

5. Read these sentences from paragraph 4 of the passage: *(blue)*

*Starfish feed on whatever is available to them. Some of their **diet** includes worms, snails, and larvae.*

What does the word "diet" mean in paragraph 4?

_____

_____

6. What is the meaning of the word "prey" in paragraph 4? *(purple)*

    a.   food

    b.   limbs

    c.   snails

69   d.   stomach

Nonfiction Text Features

Nonfiction authors use text features to help the reader understand the text.

Types of Text Features:

1. <u>Text features that are part of a text</u>
   - Shows reader how text is organized
   - Tells reader what sections are about

2. <u>Navigating text features</u>
   - Tells reader what pages to find topics or words on

3. <u>Text features that support the text</u>
   - Gives reader additional information about text

4. <u>Special print</u>
   - Draws attention to important vocabulary words

5. <u>Electronic search tools</u>
   - Helps the reader navigate computers and websites

Model

It is important to pay attention to the text features as you preview, read, or review text. Text features can guide you, so you know where to find information. Text features can also give you additional information.

Read the text below. Study the text features. What information does each text feature give you?

The Explosive World of Volcanoes

Volcanoes are fascinating natural structures that can erupt with incredible force. This short guide will explore different types of volcanoes and what makes them erupt.

Types of Volcanoes

- **Shield Volcanoes:** These are large, broad volcanoes with gentle slopes made from layers of lava. Examples include Mauna Loa in Hawaii.
- **Composite Volcanoes:** Known for their explosive eruptions, these volcanoes are tall and cone-shaped. They consist of layers of ash and hardened lava.

What Causes an Eruption?

Volcanoes erupt due to the immense pressure of hot gases and molten rock, called magma, beneath the Earth's surface. When this pressure builds up enough, it forces its way out, resulting in an eruption.

Safety Tips

In case of an eruption, keep distance, follow evacuation orders, and stay alert to from authorities.

Did You Know?

Volcano Alert Levels

Green: No immediate danger.
Yellow: Be cautious, volcano is restless.
Orange: Eruption likely, prepare to evacuate.
Red: Eruption in progress, evacuate immediately.

Text Feature	What It Shows Me
Title (red)	
Headings (orange)	
Bold Print (yellow)	
Sidebar (green)	

← →  http://www.bochesesitalian.com/ 🔍

File   Edit   View   Favorites   Tools   Help

🏠 ✉ f 📷

| Our Story | The Food | Pictures | Location |

Bochese's Italian
860-521-0983

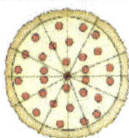

Appetizers

Salads

Pizza

Traditional Cheese

Mozzarella cheese with tomato sauce

Pepperoni

Mozzarella cheese and pepperoni with tomato sauce

Caprese Pizza

Fresh mozzarella, tomatoes, and basil with red sauce

Mushroom Mania

Fresh mozzarella, pesto sauce, portobello, button, and shitake mushrooms

Classic Dishes

Dessert

Build Your Own Pizza

Toppings

Cheeses
- fresh mozzarella, provolone, parmesan, cheddar

Sauces
- tomato, pesto, olive oil, alfredo

Meats
- pepperoni, grilled chicken, sausage, ham

Veggies
- spinach, pineapple, peppers, onions

Text Features   Name: _____ Date: _____

Answer the following questions. <u>Underline</u> the text evidence in the color indicated.

1. Where on the website can you find the address of the restaurant?

    a.   the sidebar

    b.   the email icon

    c.   the *Classic Dishes* hyperlink

    d.   the *Location* tab on the electronic menu

2. Identify a type of pizza that has fresh mozzarella, tomatoes, and basil. Then explain which two text features on this website helped you locate this information.

Type of Pizza: _____

First text feature that helped me: _____

Second text feature that helped me: _____

3. By reading the sidebar on this website, you can find out about: (Choose all that apply.)

    a.   the restaurant's phone number

    b.   toppings for building your own pizza

    c.   how to find the restaurant on social media

    d.   different types of vegetables the restaurant has for pizza

4. Which text feature could you use to find out the different types of meats you can have on your pizza?

    a.   the subheading *Meats* in the sidebar

    b.   the title of the sidebar

    c.   the hyperlink *salads*

    d.   the *Pictures* tab on the electronic menu

5. Which text feature would be most useful for finding out more about deserts offered?

    a.   the *Home* icon

    b.   the *Dessert* hyperlink

    c.   *The food* tab on the electronic menu

    d.   the *Favorites* tab on the electronic menu

73

6. What text feature could you use to email the restaurant?   purple

    a.   an icon

    b.   a hyperlink

    c.   bold print

    d.   a subheading

7. Name the different types of sauce you can have on your pizza. Then explain two text features that helped you find this information.   pink

Types of sauce: _____

First text feature that helped me: _____

Second text feature that helped me: _____

8. Where could you click to find information about the story of the restaurant?   brown

    a.   an icon

    b.   a heading

    c.   a hyperlink

    d.   an electronic menu

9. What text feature is used on the text *Appetizers*?   black

    a.   icon

    b.   Sidebar

    c.   hyperlink

    d.   electronic menu

10. If you want to go to the homepage on this website, what text feature should you click? How do you know?   blue

_____

_____

_____

74

http://www.toypalace.com/

File   Edit   View   Favorites   Tools   Help

The Toy Palace

| About Us | Specials | Gifts | Location | My Account |

SALE

Weekly Specials

Clearance

...oys: 2-4 Years

Boys' Toys
Girls' Toys
Age
birth-12 months
12-24 Months
2-4 Years
5-7 Years
8-11 Years
12-14 Years
big kids

Brand
Sale

Dump Truck
$9.99
★★★

Drum
$6.99
★★★

Train
$15.99
★★★★

Rag Doll
$10.99
★★★★

Teddy Bear
$8.99
★★★★

Sail Boat
$7.99
★★

Contact Us

Job Opportunities

Store Locator

Help

My Account

Name: _____ Date: _____

Answer the following questions. <u>Underline</u> the text evidence in the color indicated.

1. Where on the website can you find the address of The Toy Palace?   `red`

   a.   the home icon

   b.   the *Brand* hyperlink

   c.   the *My Account* tab on the electronic menu

   d.   the *Location* tab on the electronic menu

2. Identify the category of toys that is being shown on the website. Which two text features helped you determine this?   `orange`

Toy category: _____

First text feature that helped me: _____

Second text feature that helped me: _____

3. The icons will guide you to: (Choose all that apply.)   `yellow`

   a.   toys

   b.   email

   c.   social media

   d.   homepage

4. Which text feature would be most useful for finding more information about the drum?   `green`

   a.   an icon

   b.   a subtitle

   c.   a hyperlink

   d.   an electronic menu

5. List the three examples of hyperlinks that can be found on this website. What is the purpose of these hyperlinks?   `blue`

_____

_____

_____

http://www.recipediva.com/

File　Edit　View　Favorites　Tools　Help

| Meet the Diva | Breakfast | Lunch | Appetizers | Dinner | Desert |

The Recipe Diva
Original and delicious Recipes by Julie

Vegetarian

Bruschetta
Cheese Dip
Flat Bread
Hummus
Pretzels
Samoasas
Spinach Dip
Stuffed Bread
Stuffed Mushrooms
Veggie Skewers

Meat

Classic Bruschetta

Simple Appetizer Everyone will Enjoy!

Ingredients

- I large tomato
- Clove of garlic
- 10 leaves of fresh basil
- 4 tablespoons of olive oil
- Loaf of French bread

Steps

1. First, preheat the oven to 350 degrees Fahrenheit.
2. Next, slice the French bread into thin slices.
3. Brush both sides of each bread slice with olive oil.
4. Then, bake the bread for 10 minutes.
5. Meanwhile, wash the tomato and basil.
6. Chop the tomato.
7. Once the bread is toasted, remove it from the oven. Rub each slice of bread with the garlic clove.
8. Finally, top each slice of bread with tomatoes and a leaf of basil.

★★★★

Simple and easy recipe that everyone loves!

Text Features   Name: _____ Date: _____

Answer the following questions. <u>Underline</u> the text evidence in the color indicated.

1. Where on the website can you locate types of vegetarian recipes? *(red)*

    a.   the icons

    b.   the heading

    c.   the hyperlinks

    d.   the electronic menu

2. Identify two ingredients you need to make bruschetta. Then explain which text feature on this website helped you locate this information. *(orange)*

Two ingredients: _____

Text feature that helped me: _____

3. The hyperlinks will guide you to: (Choose all that apply.) *(yellow)*

    a.   social media

    b.   lunch recipes

    c.   different vegetarian and meat recipes

    d.   a way to review the recipe

4. Which text feature would be most useful for finding out about the author of the website? *(green)*

    a.   an icon

    b.   a subtitle

    c.   a hyperlink

    d.   an electronic menu

5. Which text feature would you use to go to *The Recipe Diva* homepage? *(blue)*

    a.   a title

    b.   an icon

    c.   a heading

    d.   an electronic menu

6. What text feature is used to list the steps you need to follow to make bruschetta?   ▱ purple

    a.   an icon

    b.   a heading

    c.   a hyperlink

    d.   the electronic menu

7. Write the subtitle for this recipe. Why did the author include a subtitle?   ▱ pink

_____

_____

_____

8. What type of food is being shown?   ▱ brown

    a.   lunch

    b.   dessert

    c.   appetizer

    d.   breakfast

9. Identify two types of vegetarian recipes you could find on this website. What text feature would you need to use to access these recipes?   ▱ black

_____

_____

_____

10. Name a text feature the author of the text used. Then explain why the author used this text feature.

_____

_____

_____

650L

All About Large Dog Breeds

Table of Contents

All About Large Breed Dogs

Large dog breeds make excellent pets for families. There are many types of large dog breeds with different needs and **temperaments**. Some large breeds make excellent guard dogs, while others are great helpers.

Types of Large Dog Breeds

The Great Dane

One of the largest dogs is the Great Dane. These massive dogs can weigh between 100-200 pounds. Great Danes were originally bred to be **hunting dogs**. Nowadays, their size and loud barks make them excellent guard dogs. This breed is known as the "Gentile Giant". This is because they are known to be very friendly and loving. They get along well with other dogs, animals, and people.

Great Danes require daily walks.

1

Labrador Retriever

Labrador Retrievers are traditionally hunting dogs. They were originally bred to help hunters by retrieving **game**. Labradors make excellent family pets. They are athletic and playful. This breed can also be trained to be **assistance dogs**. Labs usually weigh between 55-80 pounds. There are three colors of Labradors: yellow, chocolate, and black.

Collie

The collie is a **herding** dog. They were traditionally used to herd livestock. Collies are very active and easy to train. They can remain active all day. They are very loyal to their owners. In addition, collies are considered one of the most intelligent dogs. They weigh between 48-70 pounds. There are different types of collies. This is why their appearances vary.

Large dog breeds make excellent family pets. No matter which breed you choose, it is important to spend time bonding and training your new family member.

2

Glossary

assistance dog: a dog trained to help a person with a disability

game: wild birds or mammals that are hunted

herding dog: a dog that is able to gather a group of animals together and move them from place to place

hunting dog: a dog that hunts with or for humans

temperament: nature of behavior

3

Index

4

80

Name: _____ Date: _____

Answer the following questions. <u>Underline</u> the text evidence in the color indicated.

1. What is this book about? Which text feature tells you this?   ◀▏▎▎ (red)

_____

_____

2. Identify three dog breeds that are written about in this text. Then explain which text feature helped you locate this information.   ◀▏▎▎ (orange)

Dog breeds: _____

Text feature that helped me: _____

3. On what page could you read about Collies? Which text feature would help you find this page quickly?   ◀▏▎▎ (yellow)

Page Number: _____

    a.   the caption

    b.   the heading

    c.   the glossary

    d.   the table of contents

4. What is the meaning of the word *game*? Which text feature helped you determine this? _____

    a.   the index   ▏▎▎ (green)

    b.   the glossary

    c.   the bold print

    d.   the subheading

5. On what page could you find the word *temperament*? Which text feature helped you? (Choose all that apply.)   ◀▏▎▎ (blue)

    a.   the index

    b.   the glossary

    c.   the bold print

    d.   the subheading

6. Which text feature helps you understand how Collies were traditionally used? (Choose all that apply.)   [purple]

    a.   the subheading "Collie"

    b.   the key word "herding"

    c.   the title "All About Large Dog Breeds"

    d.   the heading "Types of Large Dog Breeds"

7. How often should you walk Great Danes? Which text feature helped you locate this information?   [pink]

_____

_____

8. Which text feature would be most helpful for finding facts about the Great Dane's size?   [brown]

    a.   the caption

    b.   the heading

    c.   the glossary

    d.   the key words

9. How is this text organized? Name two text features that helped you determine this.   [black]

_____

_____

10. Name a text feature the author of the text used. Then explain why the author used this text feature.

_____

_____

690L

Roberto Clemente

Table of Contents

Roberto Clemente
The Life and Legacy of a Hero

Childhood
Roberto Clemente was born on August 18, 1934. He was born in Puerto Rico. He was the youngest of seven children. Roberto grew up in poverty. He worked in the sugar fields to help his family. When Roberto was very young, he loved baseball. At just 16, he played baseball for Puerto Rico's **amateur** team.

The Beginning of a Career
When Roberto was 18, he was offered a contract to play baseball. Two years later, Roberto moved to Canada to play baseball with the Montreal Royals. Roberto sat on the bench most of this year.

A scout from the Pittsburgh Pirates noticed Roberto and **recruited** him the next year.

Photo of Roberto during his Major League days with the Pirates

1

Major Leagues
Roberto began playing with the Pittsburgh Pirates in 1955. He struggled with people judging him because of his race. Also, he did not know much English. Roberto stood up to this **discrimination**. He also became friends with other players who were treated unfairly due to their race.

Despite the discrimination Roberto encountered, his talent spoke for itself. In the 1960s, Roberto earned National League All-Star every year except for 1968. He also won two World Series with the Pirates. In 1971, Roberto won the World Series **MVP**.

Personal Life
In 1961, when Roberto was thirty years old, he married Vera Zabala. They had three children. Roberto spent his off-season doing charity work.

Death
One of Roberto's charity projects included helping Nicaragua after a huge earthquake. Roberto took a flight to help the survivors. Tragically, the airplane crashed. Roberto was never found. After his death, Roberto was inducted into the Baseball Hall of Fame. The Roberto Clemente Award was also created. Each year, an outstanding baseball player who is involved in the community receives this award.

2

Glossary

amateur: someone who plays a sport for fun

discrimination: treating someone differently because of their race, age, or sex

MVP: an award for the most valuable player

recruit: a new member of a group

3

Index
amateur, 1
discrimination, 2
major leagues, 2
MVP, 2

Montreal Royals, 1
National League All-Star, 2
Pittsburgh Pirates, 1, 2
recruited, 2

4

Text Features   Name: _____ Date: _____

Answer the following questions. <u>Underline</u> the text evidence in the color indicated.

1. What is this book about? Which text feature tells you this?   red

_____

_____

2. Where did Roberto Clemente grow up? Which text feature helped you locate this information quickly?   orange

_____

Text feature that helped me: _____

3. What is the meaning of the word *amateur*? Which text feature helped you determine this? _____   yellow

    a.   the index

    b.   the glossary

    c.   the bold print

    d.   a subheading

4. On what page could you read about Roberto's personal life? Which text feature helped you? (Choose all that apply.)   green

Page Number: _____

    a.   the glossary

    b.   the bold print

    c.   a subheading

    d.   the table of contents

5. On what pages could you find the words *Pittsburgh Pirates*? Which text feature would help you find these page numbers quickly?   blue

Page Number: _____

    a.   the index

    b.   the heading

    c.   the glossary

    d.   the table of contents

6. Which subheading would be most helpful for finding facts about Roberto's professional career with the Pirates?

purple

    a.   Childhood

    b.   The Beginning of a Career

    c.   Major Leagues

    d.   Personal Life

7. Explain what the caption is telling you. What is the caption's purpose?

pink

_____

_____

_____

8. What is the subtitle of the book? Why did the author choose to include a subtitle?

brown

_____

_____

_____

9. How is this text organized? Name two text features that helped you determine this.

black

_____

_____

_____

10. Name a text feature the author of the text used. Then explain why the author used this text feature.

_____

_____

85

690L

Venus
Earth's Twin

Table of Contents

Venus
Earth's Twin

Venus is the second planet from the Sun. Venus is named after the Roman goddess of love. It was named this because the planet is bright and beautiful.

Description

Venus is considered Earth's "twin planet". This is because Venus and Earth have a similar size and **mass**. Like Earth, Venus is also rocky. Unlike Earth, Venus has a very **dense atmosphere**.

The temperature on Venus is about 863 degrees Fahrenheit. This makes Venus the hottest planet in our solar system! Venus is surrounded by clouds. These clouds make it impossible to see the surface from space. Venus's surface is dry like a desert. There are more volcanoes on Venus than any other planet.

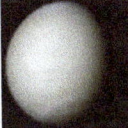

Photo of Venus taken from Mariner 10

1

Venus's Orbit

Venus **orbits** the Sun about every 225 earth days. This makes a year on Venus 140 days shorter than a year on Earth. Venus **rotates** on its **axis** slower than any other planet in our solar system. It takes 243 earth days for Venus to rotate once. This means that a day on Venus is longer than a year on Venus!

Observing Venus

Next to the Moon, Venus is the second-brightest object that can be seen from Earth. Venus is brightest when it is closest to Earth. Venus is so bright that it can even be seen during the day when the sky is clear.

Venus is a fascinating planet. Next time you are outside, try to observe Venus. There is still a lot we need to learn about this amazing planet.

Venus Facts
Distance from the Sun: 67,237,910 miles
Gravity: 0.9
Moons: None

Glossary

atmosphere: the gases surrounding a planet

axis: imaginary line that a planet rotates

dense: thick, heavy

mass: how much matter is in an object

orbit: the curved path of an object around a star, planet, or moon

rotate: to move in a circle around a center

3

Index

4

2

Text Features   Name: _____ Date: _____

Answer the following questions. <u>Underline</u> the text evidence in the color indicated.

1. What is this book about? Which text feature tells you this?   [red]

_____

_____

2. Identify one way that Earth is similar to Venus. Then explain which text feature helped you locate this information.   [orange]

Earth and Venus similarity: _____

Text feature that helped me: _____

3. On what pages could you find the word *Earth*? Which text feature would help you find these page numbers quickly?   [yellow]
Page Number: _____
   a.   the index
   b.   the heading
   c.   the glossary
   d.   the table of contents

4. On what page could you read about watching Venus from Earth? Which text feature helped you? (Choose all that apply.)   [green]
Page Number: _____
   a.   the index
   b.   the glossary
   c.   the bold print
   d.   a subheading

5. What is the meaning of the word *axis*? Which text feature helped you determine this? _____
   a.   the index   [blue]
   b.   the glossary
   c.   the bold print
   d.   a subheading

6. Which text feature is used to show the reader key words. Name two key words from the text.

    a.   the index   2 key words from the text: _____

    b.   the caption   _____

    c.   the glossary

    d.   the bold print

7. Where did the photo of Venus come from? Which text feature helped you locate this information?

_____

_____

_____

8. Which text feature would you use to locate how many moons Venus has?

    a.   the caption

    b.   the heading

    c.   the text box

    d.   the key words

9. How is this text organized? Name two text features that helped you determine this.

_____

_____

_____

10. What is the subtitle for this book? Why did the author choose to include a subtitle?

_____

_____

Author's Purpose

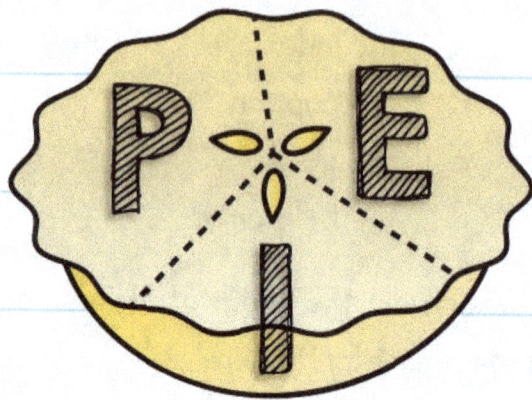

Authors write to:
- Persuade
- Inform
- Entertain

👜 When authors want to **persuade** their readers, they are trying to convince the readers to believe something. They explain why they feel the way they do.

👜 When authors want to **inform** their readers, they are trying to teach their readers something.

👜 When authors want to **entertain** their readers, they are writing for the readers to enjoy the texts.

WRITING TO INFORM

When an author's purpose is to inform readers, the author might
→ Explain something
→ Answer a question
→ Describe a person, place, or thing

89

IDENTIFY THE AUTHOR'S PURPOSE

 First, identify the **topic** of the text. Ask yourself, *"What is the whole text about?"*

 Identify key supporting **details** in the text. Ask yourself, *"What are some details that prove the topic of the text is _____?"*

 Underline any **key words** that may give you hints about the type of text you are reading.

 Use the topic and key details to determine the author's purpose. Ask yourself the following:

→ "Are the topic and key details **explaining** something to me?"

→ "Are the topic and key details **answering** a question?"

→ "Are the topic and key details **describing** a person, place, or thing?"

430L

Tying Your Shoes

Are you sick of always having to ask people to tie your shoes for you? Do you trip over your laces as you're walking? Follow these simple steps to tie your own shoes.

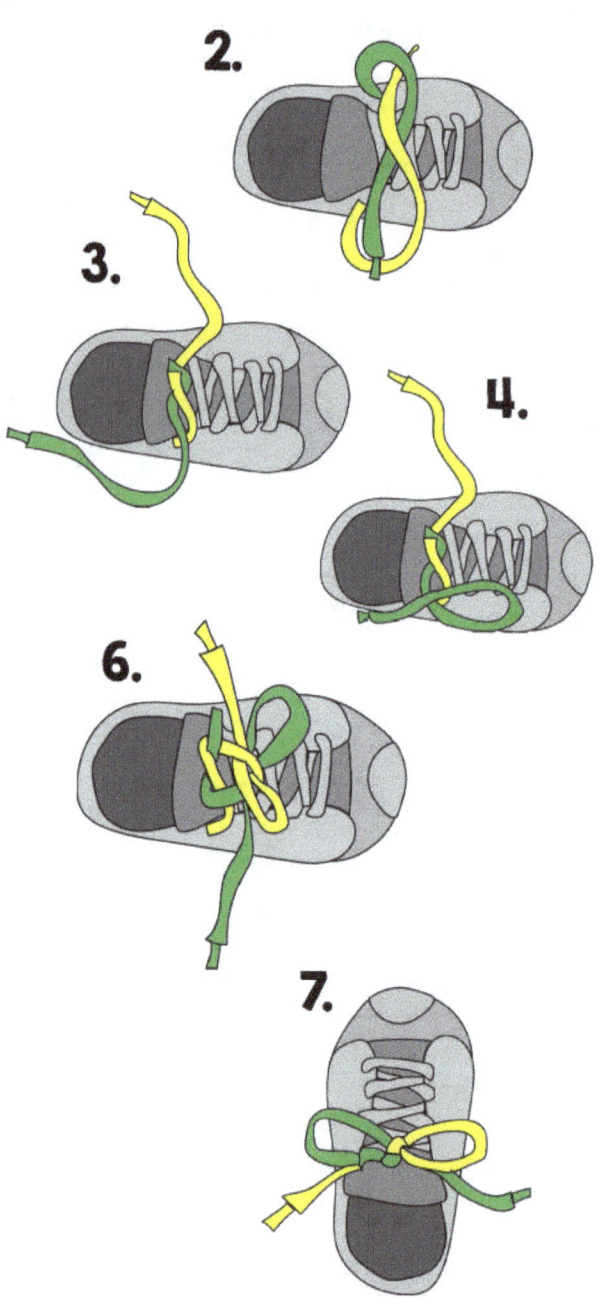

1. First, put your shoes on your feet.
2. Next, pull the laces tight. Cross one lace over the other. Loop the lace on bottom through the top of the cross.
3. Pull the laces tight to form a knot.
4. Then, make a loop with one lace, and pinch it close to the shoe with your fingers.
5. After, make another loop with the opposite lace, and pinch it close to the shoe with your other fingers.
6. Cross both loops to make an X. Pull one loop under the other.
7. Last, pull the laces tight. Your shoes are tied!

Follow these steps and you will be ready to walk confidently.

Name: _____ Date: _____

Answer the following questions. <u>Underline</u> the text evidence in the color indicated.

1. What is this passage all about?   red

_____

_____

2. What are three details that support the main topic?   orange

• _____

_____

• _____

_____

• _____

_____

3. Which of the following details could the author add to their passage to support the main point? (Choose all that apply.)   yellow

   a. Pull your laces tight so they don't come untied.

   b. There are many different ways to tie your shoes.

   c. Make loops with your laces that look like bunny ears.

   d. If you don't want your shoes to come untied, double knot them.

4. What key words help you determine the author's purpose?   green

_____

_____

_____

5. What is the author's purpose for writing this text? (What is the author explaining? What question is the author answering? What is the author describing?)

blue

_____

_____

_____

_____

6. Give two pieces of text evidence that helped you determine the author's purpose. (How did the author set up the text? Did the details and main topic lead you to the author's purpose? Did key words help you?)

purple

• _____

   _____

• _____

   _____

7. With which statement would the author most likely agree?

red

   a.   Learning to tie your shoes is easy.

   b.   It is easier to wear Velcro shoes.

   c.   Ask your parents to tie your shoes.

   d.   You must be at least six-years-old to tie your shoes.

500L

Building a Snowman

Nothing is more magical than waking up to the ground covered by a blanket of fluffy white snow. My favorite thing to do on a snowy day is to build a snowman.

First, pack two handfuls of snow together tightly until they form a ball. Next, place the snowball on the ground. Roll it until it forms a very large base (about two feet wide). Then, repeat the above steps to make a medium-sized ball (about 1.5 feet wide). Place the medium-sized snowball on top of the large snowball. After, make a small snowball for the head. Place the head on top of the medium-sized snowball. Finally, decorate the snowman. You can use sticks for arms, a carrot for a nose, rocks for eyes, and buttons for a shirt. If you would like, you can even add a scarf or a hat!

Building a snowman on a snowy day is a simple and enjoyable activity.

Author's Purpose   Name: _____ Date: _____

Answer the following questions. <u>Underline</u> the text evidence in the color indicated.

1. What is this passage all about?   red

_____

_____

2. What are three details that support the main topic?   orange

• _____

_____

• _____

_____

• _____

_____

3. Which of the following details could the author add to their passage to support the main point? (Choose all that apply.)   yellow

    a.   Your snowman can even wear gloves.

    b.   Next, you can build a whole snowman family.

    c.   Enjoy your snowman, because he will melt when it gets warm.

    d.   You need to make three large snowballs to build a snowman.

4. What key words help you determine the author's purpose?   green

_____

_____

_____

95

Name: _____ Date: _____

5. What is the author's purpose for writing this text? (What is the author explaining? What question is the author answering? What is the author describing?)   `blue`

_____

_____

_____

_____

6. Give two pieces of text evidence that helped you determine the author's purpose. (How did the author set up the text? Did the details and main topic lead you to the author's purpose? Did key words help you?)   `purple`

• _____

_____

_____

• _____

_____

7. With which statement would the author most likely agree?   `red`

    a.   It is fun and simple to build a snowman.

    b.   When it snows, you can also go sledding.

    c.   It is better to leave a snowman undecorated.

    d.   The head of a snowman should be the largest snowball.

630L

Pizza! Pizza!

Who can resist the mouthwatering smell of cheesy pizza? There is nothing like the feeling of sinking your teeth into the soft and crunchy dough. Pizza is the best food because you can make it any way that you want! Follow these simple steps to create your own delectable dinner.

Ingredients
- Pizza Dough
- Tomato Sauce
- Mozzarella Cheese
- Toppings of your choice

First, roll the pizza dough out flat, and place it on a cookie sheet. Next, brush the crust with olive oil. Then, spread a thin layer of tomato sauce over the dough. (If you like white pizza, you can use a white sauce.) After, sprinkle the sauce with a layer of grated mozzarella cheese. You can add any toppings you like. My favorite toppings are ham and pineapple. Finally, bake the pizza in the oven on 450° for 20 minutes. Last but not least, allow the pizza to cool for five minutes before you cut it into slices. Enjoy!

97

Name: _____ Date: _____

Answer the following questions. <u>Underline</u> the text evidence in the color indicated.

1. What is this passage all about?   red

_____

_____

2. What are three details that support the main topic?   orange

• _____

_____

• _____

_____

• _____

_____

3. Which of the following details could the author add to their passage to

support the main point? (Choose all that apply.)   yellow

    a.   You should eat pizza every day.

    b.   Other popular toppings include peperoni and mushroom.

    c.   After your pizza cooks, you can top it with parmesan cheese

    d.   Making your own pizza is a healthier option than ordering delivery.

4. What key words help you determine the author's purpose?   green

_____

_____

_____

5. What is the author's purpose for writing this text? (What is the author explaining? What question is the author answering? What is the author describing?)

blue

_____

_____

_____

_____

6. Give two pieces of text evidence that helped you determine the author's purpose. (How did the author set up the text? Did the details and main topic lead you to the author's purpose? Did key words help you?)

purple

• _____

_____

• _____

_____

7. With which statement would the author most likely agree?

red

a.   Pizza is very unhealthy.

b.   Homemade pizza is simple and delicious.

c.   Pizza is best if you order it from a restaurant.

d.   You could eat pizza for breakfast, lunch, and dinner.

530L

African Elephants

The African elephant is the largest land animal. A male can weigh up to 13,000 pounds. A female can weigh up to 7,000 pounds. African elephants have thick bodies and thick legs. African elephants are well known for their large ears. These ears help cool the elephants down. In addition, elephants are known for their trunks. An elephant's trunk acts as a limb. The trunk projects sounds and is also used for touch.

An African elephant grows new teeth four to six times throughout its life. A common cause of death in African elephants is losing their last set of teeth. This happens around the age of 50. An elephant's tusks are teeth. Elephants use their tusks to dig up roots and strip bark from trees for food. Tusks are also used for fighting off predators.

African elephants' ancestors have dwelled on earth for 55 million years. Their amazing features have helped them adapt and survive. African elephants are remarkable animals.

Name: _____ Date: _____

Answer the following questions. <u>Underline</u> the text evidence in the color indicated.

1. What is this passage all about?   red

_____

_____

2. What are three details that support the main topic?   orange

• _____

_____

• _____

_____

• _____

_____

3. Which of the following details could the author add to their passage to support the main point? (Choose all that apply.)   yellow

    a.   African elephants have 24 teeth.

    b.   Asian elephants are 8-10 feet tall.

    c.   Humans are the main threat to elephants.

    d.   There are two types of African elephants.

4. What key words help you determine the author's purpose?   green

_____

_____

_____

Name: _____ Date: _____

5. What is the author's purpose for writing this text? (What is the author explaining? What question is the author answering? What is the author describing?)   `blue`

_____

_____

_____

_____

6. Give two pieces of text evidence that helped you determine the author's purpose. (How did the author set up the text? Did the details and main topic lead you to the author's purpose? Did key words help you?)   `purple`

• _____

   _____

   _____

• _____

   _____

   _____

7. With which statement would the author most likely agree?   `red`

   a.   Asian elephants are fascinating to learn about.

   b.   An elephant's trunk is their most important body part.

   c.   African elephants are more interesting than Asian elephants.

   d.   African elephants have many features that help them survive their harsh climate.

560L

Fresh Chocolate Chip Cookies

There is nothing better than the mouthwatering scent of fresh chocolate chip cookies. Chocolate chip cookies are a favorite snack of many Americans. These tasty treats contain moist butter, sweet sugar, and rich chocolate chips.

You can make chocolate chip cookies any way you like. Some people prefer soft, chewy cookies. Soft cookies melt in your mouth. Others like them crispy and crunchy. You can also make a variety of chocolate chip cookies. Try adding peanut butter or cocoa powder to the dough. Some people like to add nuts to their cookies for more crunch. Most people agree that fresh chocolate chip cookies are best served with a cool glass of milk.

103

Author's Purpose   Name: _____ Date: _____

Answer the following questions. <u>Underline</u> the text evidence in the color indicated.

1. What is this passage all about?   red

_____

_____

2. What are three details that support the main topic?   orange

- _____

- _____

- _____

_____

- _____

_____

3. Which of the following details could the author add to their passage to support the main point? (Choose all that apply.)   yellow

    a.   Chocolate chip cookies should bake for 20 minutes.

    b.   Tollhouse chocolate chip cookies are the best brand to buy.

    c.   The best chocolate chip cookies crumble as you take a bite.

    d.   The ingredients you need to make chocolate chip cookies are butter, sugar, eggs, flour, baking soda, and chocolate chips.

4. What key words help you determine the author's purpose?   green

_____

_____

_____

5. What is the author's purpose for writing this text? (What is the author explaining? What question is the author answering? What is the author describing?)   blue

_____

_____

_____

_____

6. Give two pieces of text evidence that helped you determine the author's purpose. (How did the author set up the text? Did the details and main topic lead you to the author's purpose? Did key words help you?)   purple

• _____

_____

_____

• _____

_____

_____

7. With which statement would the author most likely agree?   red

   a. Sugar cookies are better than chocolate chip cookies.

   b. Store-bought chocolate chip cookies are better than homemade.

   c. You should only eat one cookie a day because they are full of sugar.

   d. There are many different ways to make delicious chocolate chip cookies.

105

710L

How Do Clouds Work?

Clouds are made up of collections of small droplets of water or ice crystals. All air contains water. Near the ground, this water is a gas called water vapor. When water evaporates, warm air rises, expands, and cools. Cool air can't hold as much water vapor as warm air. As a result, some of the water vapor condenses onto tiny pieces of dust floating in the air. These droplets of water are so small and light that they float in the air. Billions of these droplets come together to form a cloud. At times, the water droplets in the cloud become large and heavy. This causes rain to fall out of the clouds. Clouds are important in the water cycle. They help with the distribution of water on Earth.

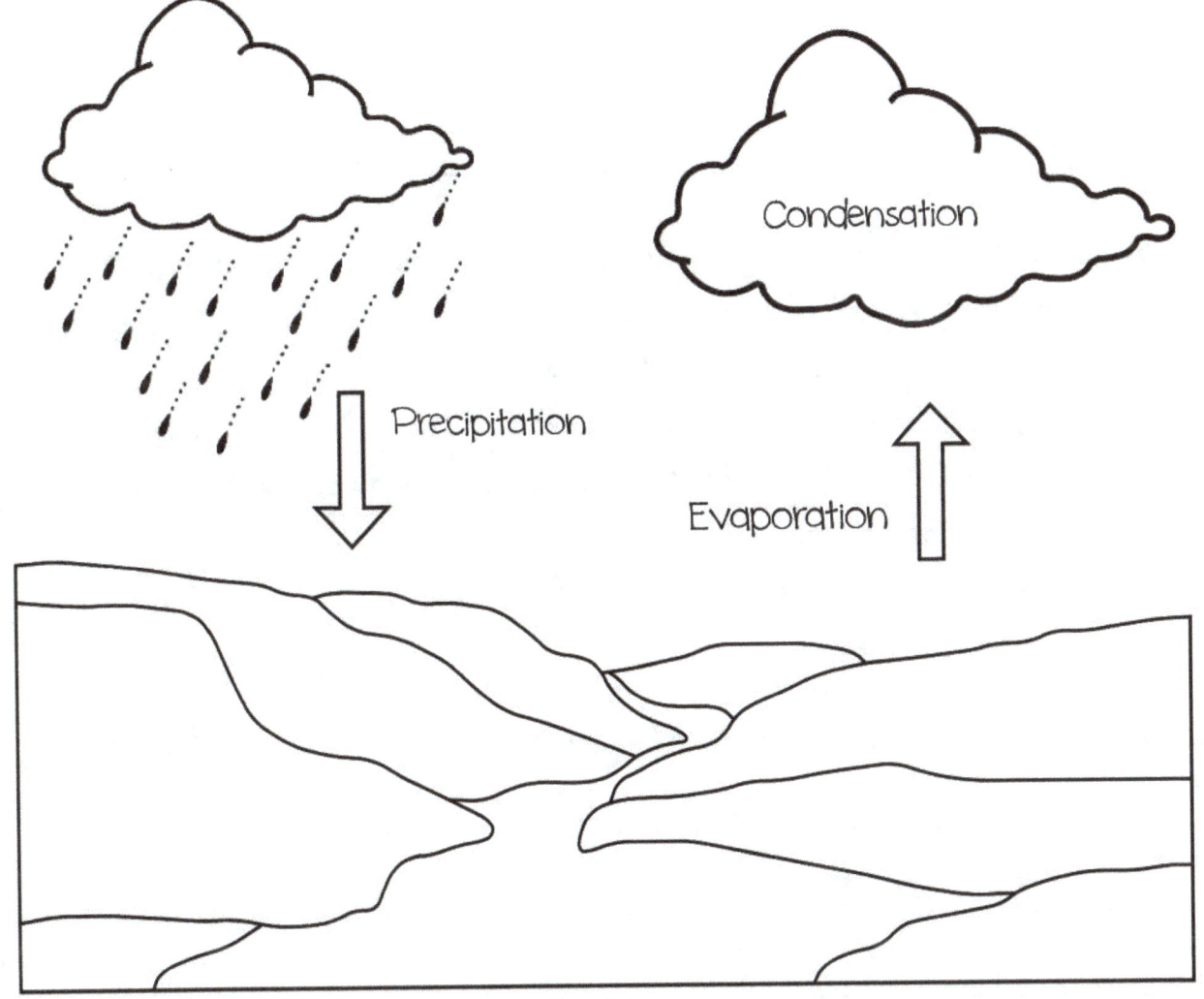

Precipitation

Condensation

Evaporation

Author's Purpose   Name: _____ Date: _____

Answer the following questions. <u>Underline</u> the text evidence in the color indicated.

1. What is this passage all about?   `red`

_____

_____

2. What are three details that support the main topic?   `orange`

- _____

  _____

- _____

  _____

- _____

  _____

3. Which of the following details could the author add to their passage to support the main point? (Choose all that apply.)   `yellow`

   a.   Cloud formation is part of the water cycle.

   b.   Clouds have different names based on their shape and height.

   c.   Cumulus clouds are fluffy, white or light gray clouds that look like puffs of cotton.

   d.   When water droplets fall out of clouds it can be in the form of rain, snow, sleet, or hail.

4. What key words help you determine the author's purpose?   `green`

_____

_____

_____

5. What is the author's purpose for writing this text? (What is the author explaining? What question is the author answering? What is the author describing?) `blue`

_____

_____

_____

_____

6. Give two pieces of text evidence that helped you determine the author's purpose. (How did the author set up the text? Did the details and main topic lead you to the author's purpose? Did key words help you?) `purple`

- _____

_____

_____

- _____

_____

_____

7. With which statement would the author most likely agree? `red`

    a.   Clouds are beautiful to look at.

    b.   Clouds can be made by people.

    c.   Cloudy days are more fun than sunny days.

    d.   The way clouds form can be explained by science.

750L

How Do Fish Breathe Under Water?

Fish are able to breathe under water because they have gills. Water has oxygen in it. Oxygen is the gas we breathe. Fish pull water in through their mouths and then use their mouths and throats to pump the water through their gills. A fish's gills have thousands of tiny blood vessels. The blood vessels take the oxygen from the water to the fish's bloodstream. After removing the oxygen, fish push the water out of their gills. Fish need less oxygen than humans and other mammals. Their gills also are larger so that they can take oxygen from water. This is why it is not possible for humans and other mammals to breathe under water. Fish can breathe underwater, which makes them different from mammals.

Name: _____ Date: _____

Answer the following questions. <u>Underline</u> the text evidence in the color indicated.

1. What is this passage all about?   [red]

_____

_____

2. What are three details that support the main topic?   [orange]

- _____

    _____

- _____

    _____

- _____

    _____

3. Which of the following details could the author add to their passage to support the main point? (Choose all that apply.)   [yellow]

    a.   To breathe underwater, you can use scuba gear.

    b.   Humans cannot breathe underwater is because they do not have gills.

    c.   Marine mammals, like dolphins, do not breathe underwater, but they can hold their breath for long periods of time.

    d.   Since fish are cold blooded, they require a lot less energy, which is one reason why they can breathe underwater.

4. What key words help you determine the author's purpose?   [green]

_____

_____

_____

5. What is the author's purpose for writing this text? (What is the author explaining? What question is the author answering? What is the author describing?)   [blue]

_____

_____

_____

_____

6. Give two pieces of text evidence that helped you determine the author's purpose. (How did the author set up the text? Did the details and main topic lead you to the author's purpose? Did key words help you?)   [purple]

● _____

_____

_____

● _____

_____

_____

7. With which statement would the author most likely agree?   [red]

    a.   Fish are the most interesting animals.

    b.   Fish are more developed than humans.

    c.   A fish's gills are essential to them being able to breathe underwater.

    d.   In the future, humans will grow gills and be able to breathe underwater.

620L

TEST: Making a Paper Airplane

Making a paper plane is a perfect activity you can do if you are bored over your summer break. Follow these simple steps to make a paper airplane that will soar.

1. First, get a sheet of regular paper.

2. Next, fold the paper in half like a hot dog.

3. Fold the top corners down to the crease in the paper.

4. Then, grab the corner of each triangle, and fold it in to the crease of the paper.

5. Last, fold each side of the plane down to make a wing.

6. After you've made your plane, you can fly it outside!

Making a paper airplane is an easy activity. With just a few folds and some creativity, you can create your very own fun.

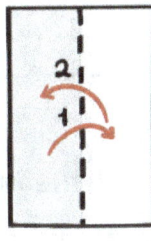
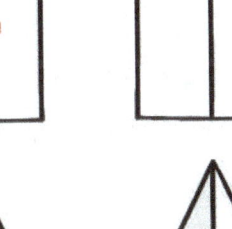

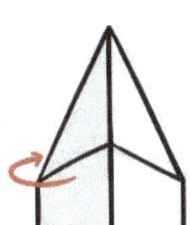

Author's Purpose   Name: _____ Date: _____

Answer the following questions. <u>Underline</u> the text evidence in the color indicated.

1. What is this passage all about?   `red`

_____

_____

2. What are three details that support the main topic?   `orange`

- _____

  _____

- _____

  _____

- _____

  _____

3. Which of the following details could the author add to their passage to support the main point? (Choose all that apply.)   `yellow`

    a.   It is best to fly your airplane on a day with a little breeze.

    b.   Before you start to fold your paper, you can decorate it.

    c.   Jack Northrop used paper airplane models to test aerodynamics.

    d.   The Chinese first invented paper airplanes over 2,000 years ago.

4. What key words help you determine the author's purpose?   `green`

_____

_____

113

5. What is the author's purpose for writing this text? (What is the author explaining? What question is the author answering? What is the author describing?) ◀ blue

_____

_____

_____

_____

6. Give two pieces of text evidence that helped you determine the author's purpose. (How did the author set up the text? Did the details and main topic lead you to the author's purpose? Did key words help you?) ◀ purple

• _____

_____

_____

• _____

_____

_____

7. With which statement would the author most likely agree? ◀ red

    a.   Blue airplanes fly better than green airplanes.

    b.   Paper airplanes fly better than wood airplanes.

    c.   You should make paper airplanes and fly them in class.

    d.   Paper airplanes are a fun activity you can do with few supplies.

730L

What Causes Colors in Nature?

Have you ever wondered why the grass is green? Why is the sky is blue? Nature has many vibrant colors.

Grass is green because it produces a pigment called chlorophyll. Chlorophyll is important in photosynthesis. Photosynthesis is the process in which plants change light into sugar. Plants such as grass make their own food through the process of photosynthesis. The chlorophyll in grass absorbs certain colors of light and sends others back to our eyes. This makes grass and other plants appear green.

The sky is blue because molecules in the air bend light. Molecules are tiny pieces of air. The air molecules break up light like a rainbow and spread blue light from the Sun downward toward Earth. Red light is spread back out into space. To people on Earth, the sky appears blue because more blue light makes it to Earth.

The earth shows us many colors because of how light reacts with the elements of science.

Author's Purpose   Name: _____ Date: _____

Answer the following questions. <u>Underline</u> the text evidence in the color indicated.

1. What is this passage all about?   red

_____

_____

2. What are three details that support the main topic?   orange

• _____

_____

• _____

_____

• _____

_____

3. Which of the following details could the author add to their passage to support the main point?   yellow

    a.   Why roses are red.
    b.   Why school busses are yellow.
    c.   A spring day is crisp and breezy.
    d.   How to mix paint colors that match the sky.

4. What key words help you determine the author's purpose?   green

_____

_____

_____

5. What is the author's purpose for writing this text? (What is the author explaining? What question is the author answering? What is the author describing?)   `blue`

_____

_____

_____

_____

6. Give two pieces of text evidence that helped you determine the author's purpose. (How did the author set up the text? Did the details and main topic lead you to the author's purpose? Did key words help you?)   `purple`

• _____

_____

_____

• _____

_____

7. With which statement would the author most likely agree? (Choose all that apply.)   `red`

   a.   It is fun to explore nature.
   b.   Colors appear due to how light reacts to objects.
   c.   The blue of the sky is prettier than the green of grass.
   d.   Science can answer many of our questions about nature.

TEST: The Grand Canyon

The Grand Canyon is one of America's most famous national parks. About five million people visit this attraction every year.

The Grand Canyon was carved out by the Colorado River. It is 277 miles long, 18 miles wide, and a mile deep. The Colorado River has been eroding the canyon for over 17 million years. The erosion has revealed layers of beautifully colored rock.

The Grand Canyon Layers

Native Americans have lived here for thousands of years. The first of the native people to inhabit the Grand Canyon were the Ancient Puebloans. Today, tribes such as the Hualapai and Navajo still live in the area.

Horseshoe Bend at the Grand Canyon

The Grand Canyon is a special place with a rich history and beautiful natural features.

Author's Purpose   Name: _____ Date: _____

Answer the following questions. <u>Underline</u> the text evidence in the color indicated.

1. What is this passage all about?   [red]

_____

_____

2. What are three details that support the main topic?   [orange]

• _____

_____

• _____

_____

• _____

_____

3. Which of the following details could the author add to their passage to
support the main point? (Choose all that apply.)   [yellow]

   a.   There are many caves inside the Grand Canyon.

   b.   Make sure you wear hiking boots to the Grand Canyon.

   c.   Horseshoe Bend at the Grand Canyon was sculpted by the Colorado
      River.

   d.   The closest airport to the Grand Canyon is Flagstaff Pulliam
      Airport.

4. What key words help you determine the author's purpose?   [green]

_____

_____

5. What is the author's purpose for writing this text? (What is the author explaining? What question is the author answering? What is the author describing?) `blue`

_____

_____

_____

_____

6. Give two pieces of text evidence that helped you determine the author's purpose. (How did the author set up the text? Did the details and main topic lead you to the author's purpose? Did key words help you?) `purple`

• _____

_____

_____

• _____

_____

_____

7. With which statement would the author most likely agree? `red`

    a.   You should go camping at the Grand Canyon.

    b.   The Grand Canyon is a beautiful sight to see.

    c.   If you go to Arizona, you should visit Phoenix.

    d.   It is best to go to the Grand Canyon when you are an adult.

Unit 3: Integration of Knowledge & Ideas

Nonfiction Text Images

Reasons Support Points

Compare & Contrast

Reading Comprehension

Nonfiction Text Images

1. Helps Comprehension

Images help the reader see what the text is discussing.

2. Shows Real Things

Photos are accurate depictions of topics.

3. Shows Details

Close ups show zoomed in images. Diagrams show parts and labels of an image.

4. Shows Data

Graphs and charts can show data in a visual way.

123

Nonfiction Text Features: Images

TEXT FEATURE	EXAMPLE	PURPOSE
Photograph		-Shows a real-life image
Caption	This is a tiny frog sitting on a bicycle seat.	-Tells what a photograph or illustration is about
Label	eyepiece, tube, counterweight, primary mirror	-Tells what a part of an image is
Close-up		-Shows what a piece of an image looks like up close
Cutaway		-Shows what something looks like on the inside
Diagram	EXTERNAL TANK, SOLID ROCKET BOOSTERS, ORBITER	-Many labels that show the parts of an image

Nonfiction Text Features: Images

TEXT FEATURE	EXAMPLE	PURPOSE
Chart/ Table		-Organizes data
Graph		-Shows data in a visual format -Different types of graphs include bar graphs, line graphs, and pie charts
Map		-Shows locations
Timeline		-Tells when events occurred -Chronological order

125

Model

It is important to pay attention to the text images as you preview, read, or review text. Text images can support information in a passage. Text images can also give you additional information.

Read the text below. Study the text images. What information does each text image give you?

Triceratops: The Three-Horned Giant of the Cretaceous Period

The Triceratops is one of the most easily recognized dinosaurs due to its three distinct horns and large, bony frill around its neck. The Triceratops lived about 68 million years ago during the Late Cretaceous period. This fascinating dinosaur roamed what is now North America. The Triceratops was a herbivore, which means it ate plants. It used its strong beak and many cheek teeth to chop up tough, fibrous vegetation. Scientists believe that its horns and frill were used for defense against predators, like the fearsome Tyrannosaurus rex, and possibly also to attract mates or recognize other Triceratops. The Triceratops has been extinct for millions of years. Its impressive skeleton, with horns sometimes over three feet long, continues to intrigue us. This dinosaur's remarkable features help us understand more about the diversity of life on Earth long before humans arrived.

Text Feature	What It Shows Me
red	
orange	
yellow	

460L

The Power of Reading

Reading is powerful. There are many benefits to reading every day. Reading improves language. Readers have a larger vocabulary than non readers. Reading increases comprehension. It improves concentration. Reading helps memory. Readers communicate better. Children develop skills when parents read aloud. Reading prepares children for school. Readers tend to do well in all subjects. Children who read make more money when they grow up. For all of these benefits, read 20 minutes each day!

Minutes Spent Reading Each Day	Minutes Read in a School Year	# of Words Read Each Year	School Days Read by the End of 6th Grade
20 minutes	3,600	1,800,000	60 days
5 minutes	900	282,000	12 days
1 minute	180	8,000	3 days

Minutes Spent Reading Per Day in Mrs. Smith's Class

```
                    X                       X
                    X       X               X
                    X       X               X
            X       X       X               X
            X       X       X       X       X
    X       X       X       X       X       X
  <—+———+———+———+———+———+———+———>
    0   5  10  15  20  25  30
```

Children read 2,151 books in 30 days in the Wild About Reading Read-A-Thon

127

Nonfiction Images   Name: _____ Date: _____

Answer the following questions. <u>Underline</u> the text evidence in the color indicated.

1. How long does the author suggest children read every day? Use the text and the text features to help you.

`red`

_____

_____

Image that helped me: _____

2. Why is it important for children to read every day? (Choose all that apply.)

`orange`

    a.   Reading improves memory.

    b.   Reading improves vocabulary.

    c.   Reading increases comprehension.

    d.   Reading prepares children for school.

3. Which statement could you conclude based on the chart?

`yellow`

    a.   If you read 20 minutes every day, you will read 900 minutes in a school year.

    b.   If you skip your reading for a few days a week, it won't affect your total reading time.

    c.   Increasing your reading time each day makes a big difference in your total reading time for the year.

    d.   There isn't a big difference in the total days you read if you read one minute per day or five minutes per day.

4. If you read 20 minutes every day, how many total minutes will you have spent reading in a school year?

`green`

_____

_____

5. How many books did children read in the Wild About Reading Read-A-Thon?

`blue`

_____

6. How many children read for 20 minutes or more per day in Mrs. Smith's class? According to the article, what could you conclude about these students?

`purple`

_____

_____

540L

The Water Cycle

Did you know that a glass of water you drink could be the same water that dinosaurs drank? Earth's water never goes away. It is constantly recycled through the Earth's atmosphere. This is why it is called a water cycle. It never ends!

Water falls to Earth as precipitation. Precipitation is rain, snow, or sleet. The water collects on land or in water on Earth. Eventually, this water evaporates. Evaporation happens when the sun heats up water and turns it into gas. The gas is called water vapor. Water vapor goes up into the air. Next, the water vapor gets cold. When it gets cold, it changes back into a liquid, which is called condensation. This is how clouds are made. When clouds have a lot of water, the clouds get heavy. Water falls back to Earth as precipitation.

The water cycle never ends. Earth's water has continued through this process for billions of years. Next time you drink a glass of water, imagine all of the places that water has been.

Condensation

Precipitation

Evaporation

129

Name: _____ Date: _____

Answer the following questions. <u>Underline</u> the text evidence in the color indicated.

1. Why is the water cycle never ending? Use the text and the text features to help you.

red

_____

Image that helped me: _____

2. What stage of the water cycle is the first photograph showing?

orange

    a.   water vapor

    b.   evaporation

    c.   precipitation

    d.   condensation

3. What stage of the water cycle is the second photograph of the clouds showing?

yellow

    a.   water vapor

    b.   evaporation

    c.   precipitation

    d.   condensation

4. Explain what happens during the evaporation stage of the water cycle.

green

_____

_____

5. In which stage of the water cycle does water vapor get cold and change back into a liquid?

blue

    a.   snow

    b.   evaporation

    c.   precipitation

    d.   condensation

6. What happens to water after it rains?

purple

_____

_____

130

600L

Arbor Day

Arbor Day is a holiday to plant and care for trees. Trees are important. They give us oxygen. Trees also give food and shelter to living things. Arbor Day happens all around the world. The first Arbor Day was in Spain. There was a big festival. It began with planting a tree. Afterwards, there was a large feast.

The first Arbor Day in America was on April 10, 1872. One million trees were planted in Nebraska. Birdsey Northrop spread the tradition of Arbor Day across the world. He brought this holiday to Japan in 1883. Soon after, he spread Arbor Day to Australia, Canada, and Europe.

Today, Arbor Day is celebrated in many countries. In Belgium, International Day of Tree Planting is celebrated on March 21. In Brazil, Arbor Day is on September 21. School children plant trees and help the environment. In China, March 12 is Arbor Day. Every Chinese citizen is expected to plant 3-5 trees each year.

It is important to remember the importance of trees every day. Celebrate Arbor Day by planting trees in your community.

Arbor Day Tree Planting in California 2011

Oak

Ash

Maple

Elm

= 10 trees

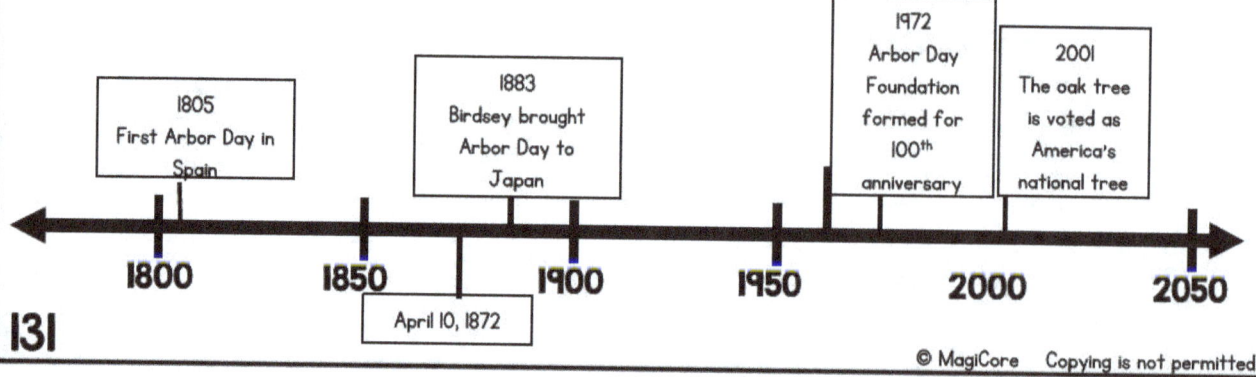

| 1805 First Arbor Day in Spain | 1883 Birdsey brought Arbor Day to Japan | 1972 Arbor Day Foundation formed for 100th anniversary | 2001 The oak tree is voted as America's national tree |

1800   1850   1900   1950   2000   2050

April 10, 1872

131

Answer the following questions. <u>Underline</u> the text evidence in the color indicated.

1. When was the first Arbor Day? How was it celebrated? Use the text and the text features to help you.

`red`

_____

Image that helped me: _____

2. Which event belongs in the timeline box under April 10, 1872?

`orange`

    a.   The first Arbor Day was celebrated in Spain.

    b.   America had its first Arbor Day in Nebraska

    c.   Birdsey Northrop brought Arbor Day to Japan

    d.   Birdsey Northrop brought Arbor Day to Australia, Canada, and Europe

3. When was the Arbor Day Foundation formed?

`yellow`

_____

_____

4. What tree was planted the most in California on Arbor Day in 2011?

`green`

_____

_____

5. How many elm trees were planted in California on Arbor Day in 2011?

`blue`

    a.   2

    b.   2 ½

    c.   25

    d.   30

6. According to the photograph, how do children celebrate Arbor Day in Korea?

`purple`

_____

_____

610L

Layers of the Earth

The earth is like an onion. It is made up of different layers. Scientists have learned about these layers by studying earthquakes and volcanoes.

The Crust

Earth's crust is the outer layer. This is where we live! It is solid and made mostly of rock. The crust is the thinnest layer. The crust surrounds both the sea and the land.

Upper Mantle

Underneath the crust is the upper mantle. The top of the upper mantle is also made of solid rock. The lower part of the upper mantle is both solid and melted rock.

Lower Mantle

The lower mantle is made of solid rock. The temperature is hot enough to melt the rock in the lower mantle, but it remains solid because there is so much pressure. When the rock in the mantel rises and falls, the crust breaks into plates. This cause earthquakes and volcanoes. Mountains and oceans are formed when this occurs.

Crust

Outer Core

The outer core is made of iron and nickel. These metals create the earth's magnetic field.

Mantle

Outer Core

Inner Core

Crust

Inner Core

The inner core is a large metal ball. It is made of iron. The inner core is 6,000 times hotter than our air. It is solid because there is so much pressure around it.

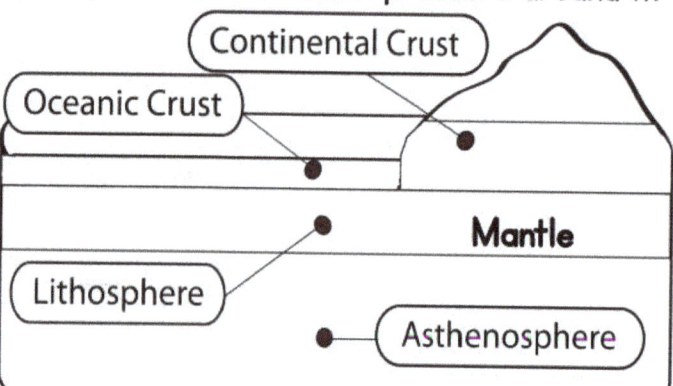

Continental Crust

Oceanic Crust

Mantle

Lithosphere

Asthenosphere

Layer	Avg. Temperature in Degrees Fahrenheit
Crust	0-700
Mantle	900-4,000
Outer Core	9,300
Inner Core	10,800

133

Answer the following questions. <u>Underline</u> the text evidence in the color indicated.

I. What are the different layers of the earth? Use the text and the text features to help you.   `red`

_____

Image that helped me: _____

2. What is the cutaway showing?   `orange`

     a.   the top layers of the earth

     b.   the names of the different layers

     c.   what the inside of the earth looks like

     d.   the temperature of the different layers

3. What is the innermost layer of the earth? Use the text and the text features to help you.   `yellow`

_____

Image that helped me: _____

4. What is the hottest layer of the earth? Is this layer a solid or a liquid? Why?   `green`

_____

_____

5. Which layers is the diagram showing? (Choose all that apply.)   `blue`

     a.   crust

     b.   mantle

     c.   outer core

     d.   inner core

6. How are earthquakes formed? Which layer is responsible for this?   `purple`

_____

640L

Bottlenose Dolphins

Bottlenose dolphins are the most common members of the dolphin family. The bottlenose dolphin is a favorite marine mammal of many people. They are known for being graceful, friendly, and intelligent.

Bottlenose dolphins are grey. They are usually 2-4 meters long. Bottlenose dolphins weigh between 330-1,430 pounds. Their habitat affects their size. Dolphins that live in warmer waters tend to be smaller. The bottlenose dolphin gets its name from its snout that is shaped like a bottle. They have blowholes on the tops of their heads for breathing.

Bottlenose dolphins live in the dark areas.

Bottlenose dolphins eat fish. They often hunt together to catch schools of fish. They are able to find fish by using echolocation. Echolocation is when dolphins release sounds and listen for the return echoes. This helps them know where the fish are located.

Bottlenose size compared to humans

Bottlenose dolphins use sound to communicate. They squeak and whistle to each other. They also use body language to communicate. They jump from the water and slap their tails. Bottlenose dolphins are very smart. Their intelligence is close to humans and apes. They are also very emotional animals.

blowhole

Bottlenose dolphins are fascinating mammals. We still have a lot to learn about these intelligent creatures.

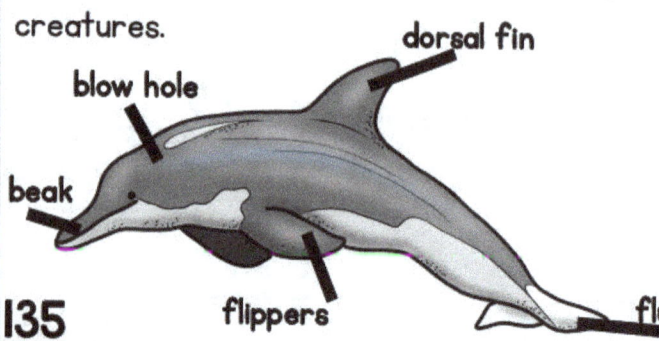

dorsal fin

blow hole

beak

flippers

flukes

135

Nonfiction Images   Name: _____ Date: _____

Answer the following questions. <u>Underline</u> the text evidence in the color indicated.

1. How does the bottlenose dolphin's size compare to a human? How does their habitat affect their size?   `red`

_____

Image that helped me: _____

2. Where do bottlenose dolphins live?   `orange`

    a.   around Australia

    b.   around the North Pole

    c.   around the South Pole

    d.   in oceans all around the world, except far north and south

3. How did the bottlenose dolphin get its name?   `yellow`

_____

_____

4. Where is the blowhole located? What is the purpose of the blowhole?   `green`

_____

_____

5. According to the article and the text features, which body part does the bottlenose dolphin use to communicate?   `blue`

    a.   eyes

    b.   heart

    c.   flukes

    d.   dorsal fin

6. Explain how dolphins catch their prey.   `purple`

_____

_____

640L

TEST: Princess Diana-
The Queen of People's Hearts

Diana Frances was born in 1961 into a British noble family. She was the fourth of five children in her family. Diana grew up in one of Queen Elizabeth II's houses. Diana always struggled in school. She loved music, swimming, and dance.

Princess Di in 1985

Diana married Charles, Prince of Wales, on July 29, 1981. Their wedding was watched by more than 750 million people on TV. It was described as a fairy tale come true. When Diana became a princess, she had royal duties. She represented the Queen at functions. She did a lot of charity work.

Charles and Diana had two sons, Prince William and Prince Harry. Diana made her children a priority. She wanted her children to experience as many normal things as possible. She took them to Disney World and McDonald's. She involved them in her charity work.

Princess Diana and Prince Charles divorced on August 28, 1996. Diana faced a lot of negative media attention after the divorce. While she was still considered a princess, Diana wanted a private life.

On August 31, 1997, Diana died in a car crash in Paris. She was mourned by people all around the world. There are numerous memorials to her. Diana lives on today through her legacy. She is remembered for her beauty, kindness, and charity work.

Memorial to Diana at the site of the car accident in Paris

Princess Diana's Life

| July 1, 1961 -Diana Frances born | 1967 -Diana's parents divorce | 1977 -Diana's dad remarries | 1977 -Prince Charles and Diana meet for the first time | June 21, 1982 -Prince William is born | Dec. 9, 1992 -Diana and Charles separate | Aug. 28, 1996 -Diana and Charles divorce |

1965   **1970**   **1975**   **1980**   **1985**   **1990**   **1995**

| 1970 -Sent to boarding school | July 29, 1981 -Charles and Diana marry | September 15, 1984 -Prince Harry is born | Aug. 31, 1997 -Diana dies |

137

Answer the following questions. <u>Underline</u> the text evidence in the color indicated.

1. When was Diana born? How many siblings did she have? Explain which image helped you locate this information.   `red`

_____

Image that helped me: _____

2. When did Dianna meet Prince Charles?   `orange`

_____

3. Which life event occurred before Diana was sent to boarding school?   `yellow`

a.   In 1977, Diana's dad remarried.

b.   In 1967, Diana's parents divorced.

c.   In 1981, Charles and Diana married.

d.   In 1996, Diana and Charles divorced.

4. What does the second photograph show?   `green`

_____

_____

5. Which of the following was an achievement of Princess Diana? (Choose all that apply.)   `blue`

a.   Diana had two sons.

b.   Diana struggled in school.

c.   Diana wanted a private life.

d.   Diana did a lot of charity work.

6. What was Diana's nickname? Which image helped you find this information?   `purple`

_____

_____

Authors Give REASONS to support their POINT ▶

POINT What the author says or thinks about the main topic. What is the main idea?

REASONS The author supports the point with details or evidence.

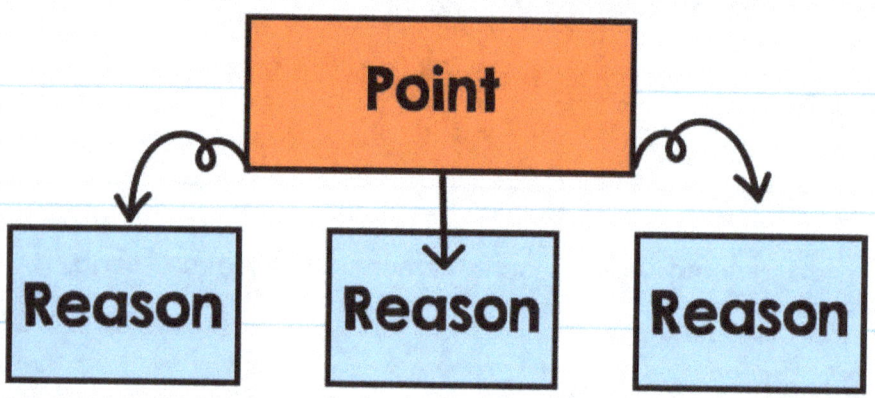

To find **REASONS** that support the author's main point:

1. Find the portion of the text where the author makes the point.
2. Ask yourself, "What reasons does the author give to support the point?"

139

Model

Name: _____ Date: _____

Read the following text. Think about the author's point. What reasons does the author use to support their point? Fill in the chart below. Underline the evidence from the text in the color shown.

Imagine a world where mountains of trash never grow and beautiful forests stay pristine. We can help make this happen by recycling! Recycling is very important for our planet. Firstly, recycling reduces waste in landfills, keeping our world cleaner. Moreover, it saves energy because making products from recycled materials uses less energy than creating them from scratch. Finally, recycling helps protect animals. When we recycle things like paper and plastic, we use fewer natural resources, which means fewer forests are cut down, leaving animals safe in their homes. So, by recycling, we help keep our planet healthy and beautiful.

Point   red

Reason   orange

Reason   yellow

Reason   green

520L

Rainy Days

There are many different types of days: sunny days, cloudy days, hot days, cold days, and snowy days. All of these days are okay, but rainy days are the best.

On rainy days, most people stay inside. There is a lot to do inside!

You can play games. You can watch movies. You can even cook food. If it wasn't raining, people would probably go outside instead of doing these fun things.

I always feel cozy on a rainy day. Wrapping up in a blanket while listening to the rain makes me feel warm and snuggly. Sometimes I have hot chocolate, which makes me feel extra cozy! It is fun to snuggle and watch movies on rainy days.

Rainy days are also good for spending time with my family. Since we're all inside together, they're perfect for talking or doing activities together. You can play games. You can build forts. There are plenty of ways to have fun together.

There are many kinds of days, but rainy days are the best.

Answer the following questions. <u>Underline</u> the text evidence in the color indicated.

1. What is the author's main point of the second paragraph of "Rainy Days"?   red

    a.   "On rainy days, most people stay inside."

    b.   "There is a lot to do inside!"

    c.   "You can play games."

    d.   "You can watch movies."

2. List one reason that supports the author's main point of paragraph 2.   orange

_____

_____

_____

3. What is the author's main point of paragraph 3?   yellow

_____

_____

_____

4. Which reason supports the author's main point of paragraph 3?
(Choose all that apply.)   green

    a.   "Rainy days are cozy."

    b.   "Wrapping up in a blanket while listening to the rain makes me feel warm and snuggly."

    c.   "Sometimes I have hot chocolate, which makes me feel extra cozy!"

    d.   "It is fun to snuggle and watch movies on rainy days."

5. What is the main point of paragraph 4?   blue

    a.   "Rainy days are a great time to spend time with family."

    b.   "There are many different types of days."

    c.   "Rainy days are for doing activities together."

    d.   "You can play games."

6. Which reason supports the author's main point of paragraph 4? (Choose all that apply.)   purple

    a.   All days are okay.

    b.   Rainy days are perfect for talking.

    c.   Rainy days are good for doing activities together.

    d.   You can build forts.

7. What is the author's main point of "Rainy Days"? Explain three reasons that support the author's main point.

_____

_____

_____

_____

_____

_____

_____

_____

143

530L

Frogs and Toads

Many people confuse frogs and toads. While frogs and toads have some similarities, they also have many differences.

Frogs and toads are both amphibians. They begin life in the water as tadpoles. As they grow, they develop lungs and live on land. Frogs and toads can be found on every continent except Antarctica. Both frogs and toads eat insects, spiders, and small fish. They catch their prey with their sticky tongues.

Tree Frog

Unlike toads, frogs live near water. Frogs have smooth skin that appears slimy. On the contrary, toads have rough, dry, and bumpy skin. Frogs' bodies are narrow, while toads' bodies are wide. Frogs' eyes are high and round. Unlike frogs, toads have lower eyes that are narrow. Frogs have long hind legs that help them jump high. Toads differ because they have shorter hind legs and take small hops. Frogs have teeth, whereas toads do not. Unlike toads, frogs have many predators. A toad's skin tastes bitter, and its smell burns a predator's eyes and nose.

Toad

Frogs and toads are interesting amphibians. Next time you see one hopping outside, try to determine if it is a frog or a toad!

Name: _____ Date: _____

Answer the following questions. <u>Underline</u> the text evidence in the color indicated.

1. What is the author's main point of the second paragraph of "Frogs and Toads"?   red

    a.   "...frogs live near water."

    b.   Frogs are similar to toads.

    c.   Frogs are different from toads.

    d.   "Frogs and toads are both amphibians."

2. List three reasons that support the author's main point of the article.   orange

1. _____

_____

2. _____

_____

3. _____

_____

3. What is the author's main point of paragraph 3?   yellow

_____

_____

_____

_____

_____

145

Name: _____ Date: _____

4. Which reason supports the author's main point of paragraph 2? (Choose all that apply.) `green`

 a. "...frogs and toads eat insects..."

 b. Frogs and toads begin life as tadpoles.

 c. "Frogs and toads are interesting amphibians."

 d. Frogs live near water, but toads do not live near water.

5. What is the author's main point of "Frogs and Toads"? Explain three reasons that support the author's main point. `blue`

_____

_____

_____

_____

_____

_____

_____

_____

_____

_____

_____

620L

Mae Jemison

Mae Jemison is an inspirational woman. She changed people's minds about African-American women and their role in science. She was the first African-American woman to travel into space. Mae has accomplished many things despite the challenges she faced.

Mae Jemison was born on October 17, 1956. As a child, Mae always wanted to be an astronaut. When Mae was in kindergarten, her teacher asked her what she wanted to be when she grew up. Mae told her that she wanted to be a scientist. Her teacher responded, "Don't you mean a nurse?" Her teacher assumed that because she was an African-American female, she could not be a scientist. Mae did not let this stop her. She studied science and nature. Mae also loved dance.

After high school, Mae went to Stanford University. She was only 16 years old. At college, Mae studied chemical engineering and Afro-American studies. Mae faced discrimination as she studied engineering. Many teachers ignored her and treated her poorly. Mae was still determined. After college, Mae got her Doctor of Medicine degree. She worked as a doctor for a few years. Meanwhile, Mae built a dance studio in her home and produced shows.

Mae at Kennedy Space Center in 1992

In 1983, Mae applied to the astronaut program at NASA. She was turned down. Still, Mae did not give up. She reapplied to NASA in 1987 and was accepted. Mae flew a space mission on September 12, 1992. She was the first African-American female to travel into space.

Today, Mae is a teacher at Cornell University. She hopes to get other minority students involved in science. Mae has also started her own companies to improve technology. Mae is an example of why you should never give up on your dreams.

Reasons Support Points   Name: _____ Date: _____

Answer the following questions. <u>Underline</u> the text evidence in the color indicated.

1. What is the author's main point of the second paragraph of "Mae Jemison"?   `red`
   a.   Mae was born in 1956.
   b.   Mae's kindergarten teacher was mean.
   c.   As a child, Mae wanted to be a scientist.
   d.   People did not believe that Mae could be a scientist because she was an African-American female.

2. Which of the following reasons supports the main point of paragraph 2?   `orange`
   a.   "Mae Jemison was born on October 17, 1956."
   b.   "As a child, Mae always wanted to be an astronaut."
   c.   "Her teacher assumed that because she was an African-American female, she could not be a scientist."
   d.   "She studied science and nature. Mae also loved dance."

3. What is the author's main point of paragraph 3?   `yellow`

   _____

   _____

4. Which detail supports the author's main point of paragraph 3?   `green`
   a.   "Mae faced discrimination as she studied engineering."
   b.   "After high school, Mae went to Stanford University."
   c.   "After college, Mae got her Doctor of Medicine degree."
   d.   "Meanwhile, Mae built a dance studio in her home and produced shows."

Name: _____ Date: _____

5. What is the main point of paragraph 4?   blue

    a.   Mae was a smart person who worked hard.

    b.   "Mae flew a space mission on September 12, 1992."

    c.   "...Mae applied to the astronaut program at NASA."

    d.   Mae did not give up when she was turned down by NASA.

6. List two details that support the author's main point of paragraph 4.   purple

1. _____

2. _____

7. What is the author's main point of "Mae Jemison"? Explain three reasons that support the author's main point.

_____

_____

_____

_____

_____

_____

_____

_____

_____

149

John and Alan Lomax

John Lomax and his son Alan Lomax were musicians. They studied music, art, and culture. They were ethnomusicologists. An ethnomusicologist is someone who studies music from the culture of the musician. John and Alan Lomax are important to American music.

Alan Lomax Playing Guitar

John and Alan were interested in American folk music. Folk music is music that is passed down from generation to generation. They traveled around the country. They interviewed folk musicians. They studied songs. They tried to figure out where songs came from. They collected artifacts that were connected to the songs. They mapped the history of many famous American folk songs.

John and Alan also recorded musicians. In the 1930s and 1940s, many folk and blues musicians didn't record their music. Many of the recordings we have from artists like Woody Guthrie and Muddy Waters came from John or Alan. John Lomax contributed his recordings and interviews to the Archive of the American Folk Song. This is found in the Library of Congress. Alan Lomax became the Archive's first employee. Both men were curators. Today, the collection has over 150,000 sound recordings and 3 million artifacts.

Lomax (left) Shaking Hands with Musician "Uncle" Rich Brown in 1940

John and Alan Lomax saved much of America's music history.

Reasons Support Points   Name: _____ Date: _____

Answer the following questions. <u>Underline</u> the text evidence in the color indicated.

I. What is the author's main point of the second paragraph of "John and Alan Lomax"?   red

    a.   "John and Alan were interested in American folk music."

    b.   "Folk music is music that is passed down from generation to generation."

    c.   "They traveled around the country and interviewed folk musicians."

    d.   "They collected artifacts that were connected to the songs."

2. Which of the following reasons supports the main point of paragraph 2? (Choose all that apply.)   orange

    a.   "John Lomax and his son Alan Lomax were musicians."

    b.   "Folk music is music that is passed down from generation to generation."

    c.   "They traveled around the country and interviewed folk musicians."

    d.   "They mapped the history of many famous American folk songs."

3. What is the author's main point of paragraph 3?   yellow

_____

_____

4. Which detail supports the author's main point of paragraph 3?   green

    a.   "They studied songs."

    b.   "John and Alan also recorded musicians."

    c.   "An ethnomusicologist is someone who studies music from the culture of the musician."

    d.   "Many of the recordings we have from artists like Woody Guthrie and Muddy Waters came from John or Alan."

151

Name: _____ Date: _____

5. What is the main point of paragraph 4?   [blue]

   a.   "Alan Lomax became the Archive's first employee."

   b.   "Both men were curators."

   c.   "Today, the collection has over 150,000 sound recordings and 3 million artifacts."

   d.   "John Lomax contributed his recordings and interviews to the Archive of the American Folk Song."

6. List two details that support the author's main point of paragraph 4.

   [purple]

   1. _____

   2. _____

7. What is the author's main point of "John and Alan Lomax"? Explain three reasons that support the author's main point.

   _____

   _____

   _____

   _____

   _____

   _____

   _____

   _____

   _____

750L

Forest Fires

Forest fires can be caused by nature or humans. Ninety percent of forest fires in the United States are caused by humans. Humans can cause forest fires by leaving campfires burning. Forest fires can also happen when people throw away lit cigarettes in the woods. Some forest fires

happen because people start fires on purpose. Ten percent of forest fires are caused by nature. Lightning can create forest fires. Also, lava from a volcano can cause a forest fire.

Amazingly, a forest fire can have a positive impact. Fire can help clean the forest floor. This helps keep the soil healthy and allows trees to grow stronger. When the forest floor is clean of brush, more shelter is available to forest animals. When the forest floor is clean, there are less plants. This means that more water can collect in streams. When these streams are fuller, other types of plants and animals thrive. Fire can help keep populations of certain trees down. This makes room for other species of trees and plants. Some trees depend on fire to release their seeds. Without fire, these seeds cannot be released, and these trees would become extinct.

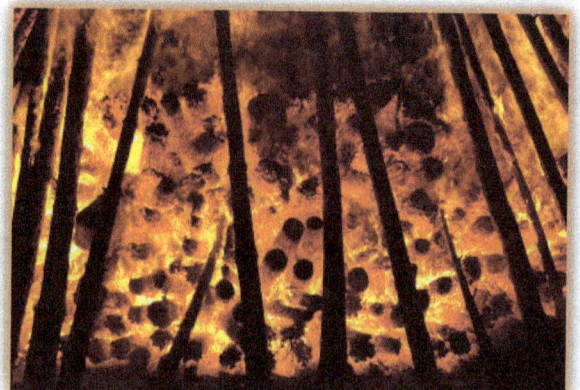

Forest fires also have many negative impacts. Forest fires change the environments in which they occur. They can destroy people's homes and animals' habitats. Forest fires also pollute the air. This pollution can harm humans.

While wildfire is important for forests, it is also a danger. It is important to monitor these fires to be sure that they are helping, rather than harming, the environment.

Reasons Support Points   Name: _____ Date: _____

Answer the following questions. <u>Underline</u> the text evidence in the color indicated.

1. What is the author's main point of the first paragraph of "Forest Fires"?

    a.   Lightning can cause forest fires.

    b.   Forest fires are caused by nature or humans.

    c.   A forest fire has a positive impact on nature.

    d.   Humans cause forest fires by leaving campfires burning.

2. List three reasons that support the author's main point of paragraph 1.

1. _____

   _____

2. _____

   _____

3. _____

   _____

3. What is the author's main point of paragraph 2?

_____

_____

_____

4. Which reason supports the author's main point of paragraph 2?

    a.   "...a forest fire can have a positive impact."

    b.   Forest fires can harm the environment.

    c.   Forest fires damage some animals' habitats.

    d.   A clean forest floor provides more shelter to some animals.

154

5. What is the main point of paragraph 3?   [blue]

    a.   Forest fires cause pollution.

    b.   Forest fires destroy houses.

    c.   Forest fires can have negative impacts.

    d.   Some plants depend on forest fires to release seeds.

6. List two details that support the author's main point of paragraph 3.

[purple]

1. _____

2. _____

7. What is the author's main point of "Forest Fires"? Explain three reasons that support the author's main point.

_____

_____

_____

_____

_____

_____

_____

_____

_____

660L

TEST: Augusta National Golf Club

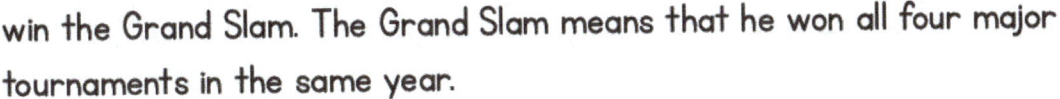

Augusta National Golf Club is in Augusta, Georgia. It has one of the greatest golf courses in the world.

Augusta opened in January of 1933. Bobby Jones designed the course. Bobby Jones was a famous golfer. He won many professional tournaments. Jones is the only person ever to win the Grand Slam. The Grand Slam means that he won all four major tournaments in the same year.

Every April, professional golfers compete in a four-day golf tournament called the Masters. The tournament is at Augusta National Golf Club. It was started by Bobby Jones in 1934. The winner of the tournament gets a green jacket. The tournament is considered a major tournament. It is the only major tournament that is held at the same golf course every year. Many people think that it is the most important tournament of the year.

10th Hole

Augusta National is very challenging. Bobby Jones was a lawyer and a golfer. He liked to be challenged. There are lots of hills and very fast greens. The course requires golfers to use strategy. Golf balls can roll from a safe place into a hazard very easily. There are even three holes named the "Amen Corner" because they are so difficult.

Augusta National is the best-maintained golf course. The greenskeepers, or people who take care of the course, work very hard. They make sure that the grass, flowers, trees, and paths are perfect. The grass is always green. There are always budding flowers on every hole.

Augusta National Golf Club is known worldwide. Its history, difficulty, and beauty have made it great.

156

Answer the following questions. <u>Underline</u> **the text evidence in the color indicated.**

1. What is the author's main point of the second paragraph of "Augusta National Golf Club"?   `red`

    a.   "Augusta opened in January of 1933."

    b.   Bobby Jones won many professional tournaments.

    c.   Bobby Jones designed Augusta National Golf Club.

    d.   The Grand Slam means to win four major tournaments in one year.

2. List one reason that supports the author's main point of paragraph 2.   `orange`

_____

_____

3. What is the author's main point of paragraph 3?   `yellow`

_____

_____

_____

4. Which reason supports the author's main point of paragraph 3? (Choose all that apply.)   `green`

    a.   The Masters was started by Bobby Jones in 1934.

    b.   "The winner of the tournament gets a green jacket."

    c.   The Masters is the only major tournament that is held at the same golf course every year.

    d.   "Every April, professional golfers compete in a four-day golf tournament called the Masters."

Name: _____   Date: _____

5. What is the main point of paragraph 4?   blue

   a.   "Augusta National is very challenging."

   b.   "Bobby Jones was a lawyer and a golfer."

   c.   "There are lots of hills and very fast greens."

   d.   "There are even three holes named the 'Amen Corner' because they are so difficult."

6. Which reason supports the author's main point of paragraph 4? (Choose all that apply.)   purple

   a.   "Bobby Jones was a lawyer and a golfer."

   b.   "There are lots of hills and very fast greens."

   c.   "Golf balls can roll from a safe place into a hazard very easily."

   d.   "There are even three holes named the 'Amen Corner' because they are so difficult."

7. What is the author's main point of "Augusta National Golf Club"? Explain three reasons that support the author's main point.

_____

_____

_____

_____

_____

_____

_____

_____

COMPARE & CONTRAST
nonfiction

Compare-
How things are alike or the same
Contrast-
How things are different

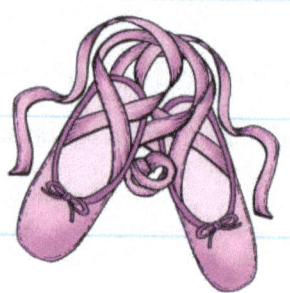

Ballet Shoes and Slippers
Ballet shoes are ==like== slippers because both shoes are types of slippers.

Ballet shoes are ==different== than slippers because ballet shoes are used for dance, while slippers are worn around the house.

To compare and contrast two different texts on the same topic:

1. First, read each article, and determine the most important points the author makes. (To determine the main points in an article, determine the main idea of each paragraph.)
2. Next, determine which points in the articles are similar.
3. Then, determine which points in the articles are different.

159

Compare & Contrast   Name: _____   Date: _____

Read the following texts. Think about the author's main point of each text. How are the points similar? How are the points different? Fill in the chart below. Underline the evidence from the text in the color shown.

The Moon's Surface

The moon, Earth's closest neighbor in space, has a surface that is both fascinating and barren. Covered in a fine, powdery dust called regolith, the moon's landscape is dotted with large holes known as craters. These craters were formed millions of years ago when asteroids and comets crashed into the moon. The surface is also home to tall mountains and deep valleys but lacks air and water. The moon's most famous feature, the Man on the Moon, is actually a pattern of craters and dark plains called maria, which can be seen from Earth.

The Moon's Phases

As the moon orbits Earth, it goes through different stages called phases, which is how it appears to change shape in the sky throughout the month. These phases include the new moon, when the moon is between Earth and the sun and we can't see it at all, and the full moon, when the moon's face is fully illuminated by the sun. Between these, there are several other phases such as the first quarter and the last quarter, where half of the moon's face is illuminated. This monthly cycle is because of the moon's position in relation to the Earth and the sun, and it repeats every 29.5 days.

	Text #1	Text #2
Main Point (red)		
Supporting Details (yellow)		

160

Name: _____ Date: _____

What to Pack for a Camping Trip

There is no better way to enjoy the great outdoors than to go camping with your family. If you pack these items, you will be able to enjoy everything the wilderness has to offer:

- A tent to sleep in
- Sleeping bags, pillows, and blankets (It may get cold at night!)
- An ax or hammer to split firewood
- Matches for a fire
- A large water jug (It is important to stay hydrated!)
- Food that will not spoil
- Trash bags (You do not want to leave your food out because you might attract wild animals.)
- Hiking boots
- Clothes for warm and cold weather

Having everything you need for your camping trip will make your time with your family pleasant. Be safe and have fun!

620L

Camping at Yellowstone National Park

Camping at Yellowstone National Park is a must for anyone who enjoys the wilderness. There are many sights to see when you camp at Yellowstone.

You can go hiking if you camp at Yellowstone. There are 900 miles of hiking trails. If you go hiking on your Yellowstone camping trip, stop at a ranger station to get information about closed areas. Make sure that you are aware of the weather before you go on a long hike. Also, carry plenty of water. Wear proper clothing.

While you are hiking, be sure to keep your eyes open for the wildlife at Yellowstone. You may see animals such as bison, bears, sheep, moose, and mountain lions. Be sure to view these animals from far away. Many animals can be dangerous if you go near them.

You can also enjoy a picnic while you are camping at Yellowstone. There are many picnic areas throughout the park. Each picnic area has tables. You can use camping stoves at picnic areas. Be sure to clean up any of your trash. Trash left out can attract wild animals.

American Bison

Yellowstone National Park is a perfect spot to enjoy a camping trip. There are many things to do while you camp at Yellowstone. You can hike the beautiful trails, watch for the amazing wildlife, or enjoy a picnic with your family.

Compare & Contrast   Name: _____ Date: _____

Compare and contrast the most important points presented by two texts on the same topic.

Answer the following questions. <u>Underline</u> the text evidence in the color indicated.

1. What is the main point of the introduction and conclusion of "What to Pack for a Camping Trip"? [red]

    a.   Camping is fun.

    b.   You need a tent and sleeping bag to camp.

    c.   It is important to be prepared for a camping trip.

    d.   Yellowstone National Park is the best place to camp.

2. What is the main point of the bulleted list in "What to Pack for a Camping Trip"? [orange]

_____

_____

_____

3. What is the main point of the introduction and conclusion of "Camping at Yellowstone National Park"? [yellow]

_____

_____

_____

4. What is the main point of paragraph two of "Camping at Yellowstone National Park"? [green]

    a.   Animals living at Yellowstone.

    b.   Tips for hiking at Yellowstone.

    c.   Activities to do when camping at Yellowstone.

    d.   Things to see and do at Yellowstone.

163

5. What is the main point of paragraph three of "Camping at Yellowstone National Park"?   `blue`

_____

_____

_____

6. What is the main point of paragraph four of "Camping at Yellowstone National Park"?   `purple`

    a.   How to use a camping stove.

    b.   Tips for having a picnic at Yellowstone.

    c.   Yellowstone is the best place to go camping.

    d.   Why you should clean your trash at Yellowstone.

7. What similar points do the authors make in both articles?   `pink`

_____

_____

_____

_____

8. How is the main point of the first article different from the main point of the second article?   `brown`

_____

_____

_____

Alexandra Scott's Mission

Alexandra Scott was born in Connecticut in 1996. She had a rare type of childhood cancer. Before Alex turned four, she decided that she wanted to start a lemonade stand. She planned to use the money she made from her lemonade stand to help other kids with cancer. Alex's first lemonade stand raised $2,000.

Alex continued her lemonade stand throughout her life. She was successful in raising over one million dollars toward kids with cancer. Alex passed away when she was eight-years-old. Alex's Lemonade Stand Foundation continues to raise millions of dollars for children who are fighting cancer.

670L

Alex's Lemonade Stand

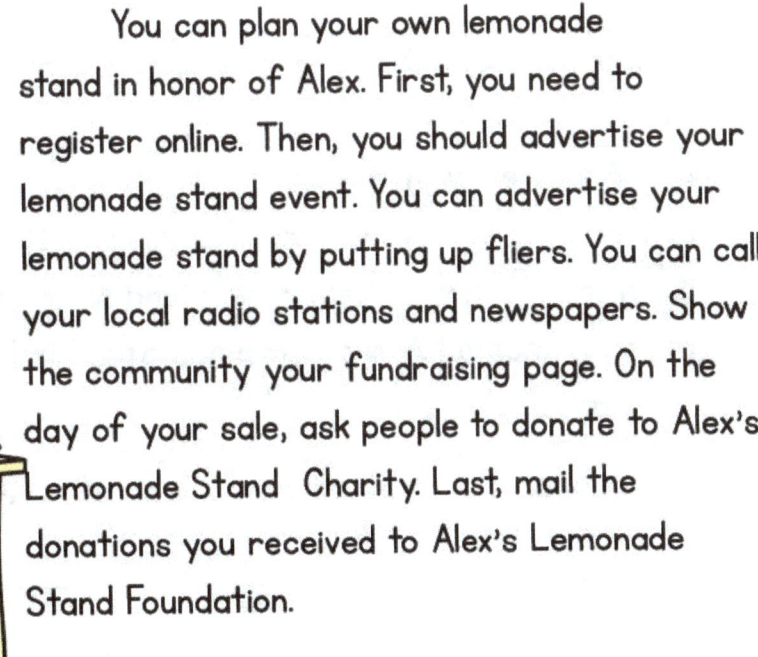

Alexandra Scott was a brave and inspiring child. She had big dreams. Alex lived with cancer. She was determined to help other children like her. Alex started Alex's Lemonade Stand when she was four-years-old. Alex passed away in 2004 at just eight-years-old.

Alex's dreams are still alive. There are lemonade stands in all 50 states, Canada, and France. A movie was made about Alex and her mission. Today, Alex's Lemonade Stand has raised over $75 million toward cancer research.

You can plan your own lemonade stand in honor of Alex. First, you need to register online. Then, you should advertise your lemonade stand event. You can advertise your lemonade stand by putting up fliers. You can call your local radio stations and newspapers. Show the community your fundraising page. On the day of your sale, ask people to donate to Alex's Lemonade Stand Charity. Last, mail the donations you received to Alex's Lemonade Stand Foundation.

Alex's Lemonade Stand is proof that anyone can make a difference in the world.

166

Compare and contrast the most important points presented by two texts on the same topic.

Answer the following questions. <u>Underline</u> the text evidence in the color indicated.

1. What is the main point of paragraph one of "Alexandra Scott's Mission"?

🖍 (red)

_____

_____

_____

2. What is the main point of paragraph two of "Alexandra Scott's Mission"?

🖍 (orange)

   a.   Alex continued her lemonade stand.

   b.   Alex's Lemonade Stand raised over one million dollars.

   c.   Alex passed away when she was only eight years old.

   d.   Alex's Lemonade Stand has been very successful in raising money for children with cancer even after Alex's death.

2. What is the main point of the introduction and conclusion of "Alex's Lemonade Stand"?

🖍 (yellow)

   a.   Alex lived with cancer.

   b.   Alex passed away when she was just eight years old.

   c.   Alex started her lemonade stand when she was just four years old.

   d.   Alex started Alex's Lemonade Stand to help kids like her that had cancer.

4. What is the main point of paragraph two of "Alex's Lemonade Stand"?

🖍 (green)

_____

_____

_____

_____

5. What is the main point of paragraph three of "Alex's Lemonade Stand"?

blue

    a.   Alex's dreams are still alive today.

    b.   You should advertise your next lemonade stand.

    c.   Ask people to donate to Alex's Lemonade Stand.

    d.   You can start your own lemonade stand in honor of Alex.

6. What similar points do the authors make in both articles?

purple

_____

_____

_____

_____

_____

_____

7. How is the main point of the first article different from the main point of the second article?

pink

_____

_____

_____

_____

_____

_____

790L

Abraham Lincoln: 16th President

Abraham Lincoln was one of the most important presidents. Abraham Lincoln was the 16th President of the United States. He was president from 1861 to 1865.

Lincoln took a stand against slavery when he became president. This caused seven southern states to leave the Union and form the Confederacy. This was the beginning of the Civil War.

First Reading of the Emancipation Proclamation of President Lincoln by Francis Bicknell Carpenter (1864)

During the Civil War, President Lincoln gave slaves freedom from slavery in his Emancipation Proclamation. Lincoln gave a famous speech called the Gettysburg Address where he said that "all men are created equal".

The country reelected Lincoln as the president again in 1864. Five days after the Union won the war, Lincoln was assassinated. John Wilkes Booth shot and killed Lincoln at a theatre in Washington.

Lincoln did not finish his second term as president. Because of his role in the Civil War, he is still known as one of the most influential presidents.

169

The Most Influential Presidents in U.S. History

Every president of the United States of America has had an impact on our country. However, most historians agree that George Washington, Abraham Lincoln, and Franklin D. Roosevelt were three of the most influential presidents.

George Washington was the first President of the United States. He was president from 1789 to 1797. George Washington was one of the Founding Fathers. He led the writing of the United States Constitution. The Constitution remains our country's laws today.

Abraham Lincoln was the 16th President of the United States. Lincoln was president from 1861-1865. He led the country during the Civil War. Lincoln is most known for making slavery illegal.

Franklin D. Roosevelt was the 32nd president. Roosevelt was president from 1933 to 1945. Roosevelt is well known for leading America through two difficult times in history. He was leader during the Great Depression and World War II.

Washington, Lincoln, and Roosevelt were three of America's most influential presidents. Without these three presidents, our country would not be what it is today.

170

Compare & Contrast   Name: _____ Date: _____

Compare and contrast the most important points presented by two texts on the same topic.

Answer the following questions. <u>Underline</u> the text evidence in the color indicated.

1. What is the main point of the introduction and conclusion of "Abraham Lincoln: 16th President"?
   a.   Lincoln was president from 1861 to 1865.
   b.   Abraham Lincoln was the 16th president of the United States.
   c.   Abraham Lincoln played an important role in the Civil War.
   d.   Abraham Lincoln is one of he most important presidents America has had.

2. What is the main point of paragraph two of "Abraham Lincoln: 16th President"?

_____

_____

3. What is the main point of paragraph three of "Abraham Lincoln: 16th President"?
   a.   Lincoln freed slaves during the Civil War.
   b.   Lincoln was president during the Civil War.
   c.   Lincoln's most famous speech is The Gettysburg Address.
   d.   Lincoln caused seven southern states to leave the Union.

4. What is the main point of paragraph four of "Abraham Lincoln: 16th President"?

_____

_____

5. What is the main point of the introduction and conclusion of "The Most Influential Presidents in U.S. History"?

_____

171

6. What is the main point of paragraph two of "The Most Influential Presidents in U.S. History"?

purple

    a.   Abraham Lincoln was an influential president.

    b.   George Washington was an influential president.

    c.   George Washington was president from 1789–1797.

    d.   George Washington was one of the Founding Fathers of the United States.

7. What is the main point of paragraph three of "The Most Influential Presidents in U.S. History"?

pink

_____

_____

8. What is the main point of paragraph four of "The Most Influential Presidents in U.S. History"?

brown

_____

_____

9. What similar points do the authors make in both articles?

black

_____

_____

_____

_____

10. How is the main point of the first article different from the main point of the second article?

blue

_____

_____

READING COMPREHENSION
Good Readers:

1. Read the whole text through.

2. Ask yourself: "What was this text about?"

3. If you know what the text was about, you are ready to answer the questions. If you have trouble summarizing the text, you need to reread until you comprehend.

4. Read each question. Circle and underline key words.

5. Search for the answer or text evidence that supports the answer. Underline it in the text.

6. Check your work!

Open Ended Response Questions:

- Restate the question.
- Answer in a complete sentence.
- Use text evidence to support your thinking.

Multiple Choice Questions:

- Go through all choices.
- Eliminate any choices that do not make sense.

480L

The Effects of Sun

There is nothing more relaxing than a day at the beach. People love to lie in the sun. Too much sun can be dangerous. It can cause a sunburn.

Sunburn is when your skin gets burned from too much ultraviolet radiation. The ultraviolet radiation comes from the sun. A sunburn causes skin to turn red. It is painful. Skin will feel hot. A person may feel tired and dizzy. Eventually the skin may peel. Severe sunburn can cause blisters. People who get severe sunburn may need to go to the hospital. Repeated sunburns may cause skin tumors. These skin tumors can be cancerous.

Anyone can get a sunburn. People with lighter skin have a greater risk. Children under six and adults older than sixty are more sensitive to the sun. The strength of the sun depends on the time of day. From 10am to 4pm the sun is the strongest. The sun is also strongest on sunny days.

You can prevent sunburn. Always wear sunscreen when outdoors. Cover your skin with protective clothing. Hats can protect your head and face. Sunglasses protect your eyes. These precautions will protect you from the sun.

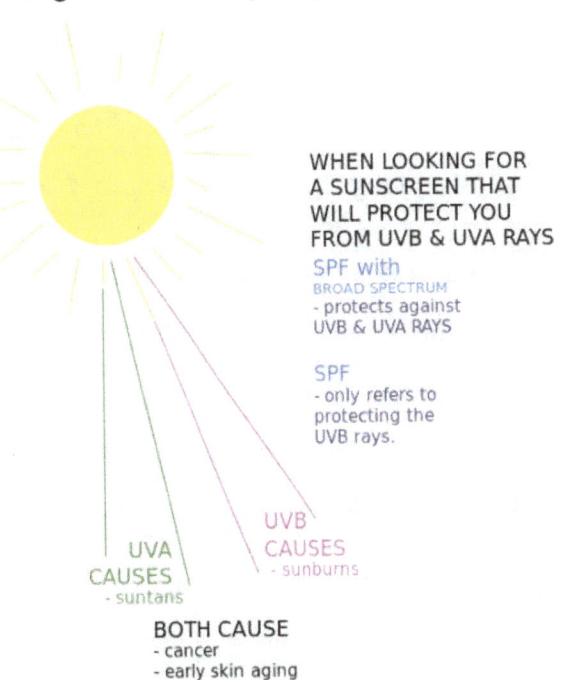

WHEN LOOKING FOR A SUNSCREEN THAT WILL PROTECT YOU FROM UVB & UVA RAYS

SPF with BROAD SPECTRUM
- protects against UVB & UVA RAYS

SPF
- only refers to protecting the UVB rays.

UVB CAUSES
- sunburns

UVA CAUSES
- suntans

BOTH CAUSE
- cancer
- early skin aging

Answer the following questions. <u>Underline</u> the text evidence in the color indicated.

1. What is the effect of too much sun?   `red`

    a.   a sunburn

    b.   a relaxing day at the beach

    c.   children are more sensitive to the sun

    d.   ultraviolet radiation comes from the sun

2. What is the main idea of this article?   `orange`

    a.   Anyone can get a sunburn.

    b.   A day at the beach is relaxing.

    c.   A sunburn has negative effects.

    d.   The sun is strongest from 10am to 4 pm.

3. What might happen if someone has many sunburns throughout their life?   `yellow`

_____

_____

4. Read these sentences from paragraph 4 of the passage.   `green`

Hats can protect your head and face. Sunglasses can protect your eyes. These precautions will protect you from the sun.

What does the word "precautions" mean in paragraph 4?

    a.   being foolish

    b.   being unsafe

    c.   being careful after something dangerous happens

    d.   being careful before something dangerous happens

5. What type of sun rays cause suntans? What else do these rays cause?   `blue`

_____

_____

Name: _____ Date: _____

6. What is the author's purpose for writing this text? (What is the author explaining, what question is the author answering, or what is the author describing?) Use text evidence to support your thinking.   🖍️ purple

_____

_____

_____

_____

_____

_____

7. What might happen to someone with severe sunburn? (Choose all that apply.)   🖍️ pink

    a.   Severe sunburn may cause a person to tan.

    b.   Severe sunburn may cause a person's skin to blister.

    c.   Severe sunburn may cause a person to go to the hospital

    d.   Severe sunburn may cause a person to turn blue or purple.

8. How did the author organize this text?   🖍️ brown

    a.   The author tells the causes and effects of sunburns.

    b.   The author compares and contrasts UVA and UVB rays.

    c.   The author explains why people should never go in the sun.

    d.   The author tells the reader the sequence of events that happens if you get a sunburn.

490L

How to Make Tacos

Are you looking for a simple and delicious meal? Tacos are a quick and easy dinner. They will please the entire family!

<u>Ingredients</u>

- 1 pound of ground beef or ground turkey
- 1 package of taco shells
- 1 pound of shredded cheddar cheese
- 1 onion
- 1 tablespoon of butter
- 2 cups of chopped lettuce
- 1 can of black beans
- Chili powder
- Salsa
- Sour cream

1. First, chop the onion. Melt butter in a frying pan. Place the chopped onion in the frying pan and cook on low heat for 10 minutes.
2. Next, add the ground beef. Cook until the ground beef is cooked through. While the ground beef is cooking, drain and rinse the beans.
3. Drain the ground beef.
4. Then, add the beans to the ground beef.
5. Sprinkle plenty of chili powder on the beef and beans. Stir thoroughly.
6. Finally, set a taco shell on a plate. Add cheese to the bottom. Scoop beef mix on top of the cheese. Top with lettuce, salsa, and sour cream.

Have your family build their own tacos! You can even start a new tradition like "Taco Tuesday."

Comprehension   Name: _____ Date: _____

Answer the following questions. <u>Underline</u> the text evidence in the color indicated.

1. What do you do before you melt butter in a frying pan ?   `red`
   a. chop an onion
   b. drain the beans
   c. cook the ground beef
   d. set the taco shell on the plate

2. What is the main idea of this article?   `orange`
   a. Making tacos is easy.
   b. Everyone loves tacos.
   c. Tacos are the best dinner.
   d. Beef tacos are better than turkey tacos.

3. What would happen if you skipped step 5?   `yellow`

   _____

   _____

4. Read these sentences from the last paragraph of the passage.
   You can even start a new tradition like "Taco Tuesday."
   What does the word "tradition" mean in the last paragraph?   `green`
   a. something you dislike
   b. something you never do
   c. something you try one time
   d. something you do over and over

5. What should you do at the same time the ground beef is cooking?   `blue`

   _____

   _____

6. What is the author's purpose for writing this text? (What is the author explaining, what question is the author answering, or what is the author describing?) Use text evidence to support your thinking.   `purple`

_____

_____

_____

_____

_____

_____

7. What should you do after you season the ground beef?   `pink`
   a.   Set a taco shell on a plate
   b.   Add beans to the ground beef.
   c.   Stir the seasoning into the beef.
   d.   Top your taco with lettuce, salsa, and sour cream.

8. How did the author organize this text?   `brown`
   a.   The author compares beef and turkey tacos.
   b.   The author explains how to start a family tradition.
   c.   The author tells the reader why tacos are the best meal.
   d.   The author tells the reader the steps you need to follow to make tacos.

179

520L

Lions and Tigers! Oh My!

Lions and Tigers are amazing animals. Both lions and tigers are part of the cat family. They are about 5 feet tall. Lions and tigers have sharp claws that retract. They also have sharp fangs and powerful legs. The coats of lions and tigers look different, but both coats help camouflage them from their prey. Lions and tigers are at the top of the food chain. Their only threat is humans. Humans threaten both of these big cats because they hunt them. They also destroy their habitat. Also, lions and tigers both have a loud roar. Their roar is used to communicate.

Lions and tigers look different. Lions are a golden color. Male lions have manes. Bengal tigers are orange with black stripes. Lions live in the African Savannah. Tigers live in jungles in Asia. Lions can live from 10-14 years. On the other hand, tigers usually live between 20-26 years. Lions weigh 250-550 pounds, while tigers weigh up to 670 pounds. Tigers are the largest cat species in the world. The Bengal Tiger makes up for 80% of the tiger species. Tigers are on the Endangered Species List. Most living tigers are in captivity. The population of lions is decreasing, but they are not yet endangered. Tigers tend to be more aggressive than lions. Lions are thought to be lazy. Lions live in prides, or groups. To the contrary, tigers live on their own. They also hunt on their own. Female lions hunt for food for their pride.

Lions and tigers are amazing big cats. They have many similarities and differences.

Answer the following questions. <u>Underline</u> the text evidence in the color indicated.

1. Where do lions live? (Choose all that apply.)   red
    a. Asia
    b. jungle
    c. Africa
    d. savannah

2. What is the main idea of this article?   orange
    a. Tigers are more interesting than lions.
    b. Lions and tigers are part of the cat family.
    c. Lions and tigers are both threatened by humans.
    d. Lions and tigers have similarities and differences.

3. What animal is shown in the first photograph?   yellow
    a. a male lion
    b. a male tiger
    c. a female lion
    d. a female tiger

4. Read these sentences from paragraph 2 of the passage.   green
The population of lions is decreasing, but they are not endangered yet.
What does the word "decreasing" mean in paragraph 2?
    a. rising
    b. growing
    c. shrinking
    d. staying the same

5. How are ions and tigers similar? (Choose all that apply.)   blue
    a. Lions and tigers are gold.
    b. Lions and tigers are camouflaged.
    c. Lions and tigers have strong legs.
    d. Lions and tigers have the same coats.

181

6. How are lions and tigers different? Use at least 2 examples from the text to support your answer.

purple

_____

_____

_____

_____

7. What is the author's purpose for writing this text? (What is the author explaining, what question is the author answering, or what is the author describing?) Use text evidence to support your thinking.

pink

_____

_____

_____

_____

8. How did the author organize the first paragraph of this text?

brown

a.   The author compares lions and tigers.

b.   The author explains how to save lions and tigers.

c.   The author tells the difference between lions and tigers.

d.   The author explains reasons why lions and tigers are endangered.

530L

Dear Mr. Saunders,

Our class has been working very hard this year. We have put our best effort into all of our work. You were so proud of us when we improved our reading levels. Most of us work hard studying at home. We complete our homework. I believe we deserve extra recess.

If we have extra recess, we will be refreshed for learning. Extra play time means more time for us to get our energy out. Also, we will spend less time talking in class. Recess will give us plenty of time to chat with our friends.

Extra recess will also give you a break! We know teaching us takes a lot of energy. You deserve a break. During recess you can have time to relax. You can also talk to other teachers.

In addition, extra recess will provide more time for kids to do make-up work. By the time we get outside, recess is almost over. Kids who didn't do their homework or who have make-up work to do can't get caught up. If you extend our recess time, kids will have more time to complete their work!

Please consider how extra recess would be beneficial. Having more recess time is a win-win situation for everyone involved!

Sincerely,

Jimmy Jones

183

Answer the following questions. <u>Underline</u> the text evidence in the color indicated.

1. Who wrote this letter?   `red`

    a.   a parent

    b.   a teacher

    c.   a student

    d.   a principal

2. What is the main idea of this article?   `orange`

    a.   Mr. Saunders is very proud of his class.

    b.   The children in Mr. Saunder's class work very hard.

    c.   The children in Mr. Saunder's class should have more recess.

    d.   Recess is the most important part of the school day for kids.

3. What reasons does the other give to support their thinking?   `yellow`

_____

_____

_____

_____

_____

4. Read these sentences from paragraph 2 of the passage.   `green`

If we have extra recess, we will be refreshed for learning. Extra play time means more time for us to get our energy out.

What does the word "refreshed" mean in paragraph 2?

    a.   tired

    b.   rested

    c.   excited

    d.   energetic

5. What is the author's viewpoint? Do you agree or disagree with the author? Why? Use your own reasons to support your answer. 🖍 blue

_____

_____

_____

_____

_____

_____

6. Which detail would support the main idea of this letter? 🖍 purple

   a.   Extra recess gives children more exercise.

   b.   Teachers work hard and should get paid more.

   c.   Students that work hard should get treats at school.

   d.   School is work for kids, so kids should get paid to go to school.

7. How did the author organize this text? 🖍 pink

   a.   The author explains how to get more recess.

   b.   The author gives reasons that support their opinion.

   c.   The author compares and contrasts having recess and no recess.

   d.   The author tells the reader the sequence of steps to get more recess.

680L

Test: Laura Ingalls Wilder

Laura Ingalls was born on February 7, 1867, in Wisconsin. She was the second daughter to her parents. She was one of five children. Laura and her family were pioneers. They moved from Wisconsin when she was two years old. They settled in Kansas in Indian country. The family soon moved again. Their home was located on an Indian reservation that they were not supposed to inhabit. The Ingalls family continued to move around the West for years to come.

Laura with her two sisters.
Left to Right: Carrie, Mary, Laura

Laura in 1885

Eventually, the Ingalls ended up in De Smet, South Dakota. The Ingalls watched De Smet grow from a prairie into a town. Laura went to school in De Smet. Just before Laura turned sixteen, she became a teacher. Three years later, Laura married Almanzo Wilder. She stopped teaching. Soon after, Laura and Almanzo had a daughter they named Rose.

The Wilder family had many disasters strike them. Almanzo get very sick and lost the use of his legs. He eventually recovered. Their baby boy passed away. They also lost their home in a fire. Laura and Almanzo moved around a few times until they settled down in Missouri.

Almanzo's parents purchased a log cabin for the couple. Laura and Almanzo expanded the house and built a farm. They grew fruit and produced poultry and dairy. Laura became a writer and editor for the newspaper named Missouri Ruralist.

Laura's daughter Rose became a very successful writer. She helped support her parents. The Stock Market Crash of 1929 wiped out the Wilders' and Rose's savings.

Laura and Almanzo

Laura decided to write an autobiography of her pioneer days in hopes of earning money. Laura's first book was titled *Little House in the Big Woods*. This book is about Laura's early childhood in Wisconsin. *Little House in the Big Woods* was very successful. Laura went on to write numerous other books about her life. The success of Laura's *Little House* books helped her family recover from The Stock Market Crash. Laura also earned many honors for her books.

Laura and Almanzo continued to live at Rocky Ridge Farm. Many fans came to meet Laura in her final years of life. Almanzo passed away when he was 92 years old. Laura continued to live on the farm for eight more years. Laura died three days after her 90th birthday. Her farm became a museum. The *Little House* books were turned into a popular television show. Laura and her family's legacy lives on today through her books and television show.

Rocky Ridge Farm

Comprehension   Name: _____ Date: _____

Answer the following questions. <u>Underline</u> the text evidence in the color indicated.

1. Why did the Ingalls family move from Kansas?   red

    a.   They were pioneers.

    b.   Laura turned two years old.

    c.   They continued to move west.

    d.   They accidentally settled on an Indian reservation.

2. What is the main idea of this article?   orange

    a.   Laura was one of five children.

    b.   Laura Ingalls Wilder died when she was 90

    c.   Laura married Almanzo and had a daughter named Rose.

    d.   Laura Ingalls Wilder was a pioneer who wrote books about her life.

3. What event led to Laura marrying Almanzo?   yellow

_____

_____

4. Read these sentences from paragraph 1 of the passage.   green

Laura and her family were pioneers. They moved from Wisconsin when she was two years old.

What does the word "pioneers" mean in paragraph 1?

    a.   people who are teachers

    b.   people who have five children

    c.   people who explore and settle new areas

    d.   people who move when they are two years old

5. What are the names of two of Laura's sisters? Explain how you located this information.   blue

_____

_____

6. What is the author's purpose for writing this text? (What is the author explaining, what question is the author answering, or what is the author describing?) Use text evidence to support your thinking.   `purple`

_____

_____

_____

_____

_____

_____

_____

7. Why did Laura write the *Little House* books?   `pink`

   a.   Laura's daughter Rose was a writer.

   b.   Laura earned many honors for her books.

   c.   Laura wanted her books to be turned into a television show about her life.

   d.   Laura hoped she could make money to help her family recover from the Stock Market Crash.

8. What happened after Laura's death? (Choose all that apply.)   `brown`

   a.   Many fans came to meet Laura.

   b.   Rocky Ridge Farm became a museum.

   c.   Laura's husband Almanzo passed away.

   d.   Laura's books were turned into a television show.

CREDITS

https://commons.wikimedia.org/wiki/File:Helen_Keller_Birthplace_House.jpg

https://commons.wikimedia.org/wiki/File:Great_white_shark_size_comparison.svg

https://commons.wikimedia.org/wiki/File:Loggerhead_sea_turtle.jpg

https://commons.wikimedia.org/wiki/File:Ryan_Hreljac_speaking.jpg

https://commons.wikimedia.org/wiki/File:Asterias_rubens_(eating).jpg

http://melonheadzillustrating.blogspot.com/

https://commons.wikimedia.org/wiki/File:Lucia-13.12.06.jpg

http://melonheadzillustrating.blogspot.com/

https://www.teacherspayteachers.com/Store/The-Painted-Crow

By User PerryPlanet [CC BY-SA 2.5 (http://creativecommons.org/licenses/by-sa/2.5)], via Wikimedia Commons

Kurzon [GFDL (http://www.gnu.org/copyleft/fdl.html) or CC-BY-SA-3.0 (http://creativecommons.org/licenses/by-sa/3.0/)], via Wikimedia

See page for author [CC BY-SA 3.0 (http://creativecommons.org/licenses/by-sa/3.0)], via Wikimedia Commons

Korea.net / Korean Culture and Information Service (Photographer name) [CC BY-SA 2.0 (http://creativecommons.org/licenses/by-sa/2.0)], via Wikimedia Commons

https://commons.wikimedia.org/wiki/File:Alex_Scott_at_Lemonade_Stand.jpg

https://commons.wikimedia.org/wiki/File:Magic_Kingdom_-_The_'27Big_Bang'27_at_Wishes_-_by_hyku.jpg

By TimothyMN [CC BY-SA 3.0 (http://creativecommons.org/licenses/by-sa/3.0)], via Wikimedia Commons

By Nhobgood Nick Hobgood (Own work) [CC BY-SA 3.0 (http://creativecommons.org/licenses/by-sa/3.0) or GFDL (http://www.gnu.org/copyleft/fdl.html)], via Wikimedia Commons

By Vxb(Own work) [CC BY-SA 3.0 (http://creativecommons.org/licenses/by-sa/3.0)], via Wikimedia Commons

By Paulo Ordoveza from Washington, DC (Chocolate World Uploaded by clusternote) [CC BY 2.0 (http://creativecommons.org/licenses/by/2.0)], via Wikimedia Commons

By GRPH3B18 (Own work) [CC BY-SA 3.0 (http://creativecommons.org/licenses/by-sa/3.0)], via Wikimedia Commons

DFID - UK Department for International Development

https://commons.wikimedia.org/wiki/File:Malala_Yousafzai_2015.jpg

ANSWER KEY

To access the answer key for the activities in this workbook, please scan the QR code with any device. The answer key will open as a PDF. For the optimal experience, please ensure you have the most up to date PDF software installed on your device.

You can tear out this page prior to distributing the workbooks to students.

190

www.ingramcontent.com/pod-product-compliance
Lightning Source LLC
Chambersburg PA
CBHW080840120626

46553CB00009B/2512